Scott Foresman
Assessment Handbook

Reading STREET

Grades 3-6

PEARSON

Scott Foresman

Editorial Offices: Glenview, Illinois • Parsippany, New Jersey • New York, New York
Sales Offices: Boston, Massachusetts • Duluth, Georgia • Glenview, Illinois
Coppell, Texas • Sacramento, California • Mesa, Arizona

ISBN: 0-328-11780-3
Copyright © Pearson Education, Inc.

7 8 9 10 V001 14 13 12 11 10 09 08 07

Contents

© Pearson Education

Chapter 4 Assessment of English Language Learners

Chapter 5 Grading

Scott Foresman Reading Street Assessment

Some Questions and Answers

This *Assessment Handbook* will be a resource throughout the school year. The handbook presents an overview of our assessment program, and it provides numerous resources in English and in Spanish that you may use to best fit your assessment, instruction, and learning goals. In addition, the *Assessment Handbook* may be regarded as a professional development resource. Inside you will find:

- guidance for using a variety of formal tests and classroom-based assessments;
- proven methods and models for assessing, evaluating, and grading children's work;
- steps for designing quality assessments in all content areas; and
- instructional strategies for preparing students for high-stakes tests.

Scott Foresman Reading Street assessments reflect current theories of teaching language and literacy, and are aligned with solid classroom teaching practices. Formal and informal assessments, combined with "assessable moments" during instruction, become a continuous cycle in which one is always informing and supporting the other, resulting in a seamless learning program for the students.

Following are some commonly asked questions about the *Scott Foresman Reading Street* Assessment Program.

How was the *Scott Foresman Reading Street* formal assessment program developed?

All of the formal assessment components of *Scott Foresman Reading Street* were developed by a specialized testing agency, Beck Evaluation & Testing Associates, Incorporated (BETA). Scott Foresman authorial and editorial staff guided these development activities with respect to specifying the purposes to be served by each component, their general content coverage, and so forth. In addition, Scott Foresman editorial teams critiqued and approved the test specifications and prototype test items for each program element. Finally, Scott Foresman reviewed and provided editorial reactions to all test content. However, the development of all materials was the responsibility of BETA, which also designed and implemented the several field-test or "validation" activities associated with several of the assessment components.

BETA is one of the country's most experienced assessment-development corporations. Over the past twenty years, BETA staff have provided standardized test content for a broad range of state and federal agencies in addition to most leading test and textbook publishers. BETA has played key roles in developing large-scale, high-stakes testing programs in over 20 states. BETA staff regularly assist state departments of education and federal agencies on matters of test development and implementation and on psychometrics, providing such consultation to over

33 state Departments of Education. Over the past decade, BETA has developed over 82,000 test items for use in large-scale assessment programs. Most of these programs include the assessment of elementary reading and other language arts. In addition, BETA professionals have facilitated the establishing of student performance standards for 16 state-level assessment programs.

All test items developed by BETA are written by experienced test-development professionals, all with extensive experience at creating test questions in the appropriate content areas and for the targeted grade levels. Most BETA writers have current or prior teaching experience; all writers participating in the *Scott Foresman Reading Street* development activities have several years of experience with test-development activities. BETA editorial staff is made up of highly experienced professionals with advanced degrees and/or certification in reading or language arts. The BETA development activities in support of *Scott Foresman Reading Street* were directed by BETA's senior staff members.

Development activities for this project began with a thorough review of the program scope and components by Michael Beck, BETA's president, and Sheila Potter, BETA's Director of Curriculum Services. This review included a study of program components from the predecessor edition of the *Scott Foresman Reading* series as well as plans and prototype materials being evolved for *Scott Foresman Reading Street*. The same two senior staff members participated in discussions with the publisher's senior staff members and their authorial team to review plans for the assessment materials and fine-tune the purposes to be served by the various assessment components. On the basis of this study and series of discussions, BETA outlined the several interrelated assessment publications and began the process of developing test specifications and prototype exercises for each product. Following iterations of review and revision based on comments by senior Scott Foresman editorial personnel, item development began. All test items were written specifically for *Scott Foresman Reading Street;* none were repeated from earlier Scott Foresman reading programs or drawn from generic "item banks." All BETA-developed items were reviewed and edited by two experienced BETA staff members before submission to Scott Foresman editorial review. Based on Scott Foresman's internal editorial review and suggestions, BETA staff then made any required revisions to the materials before they were produced.

There are two critical elements of the assessment-development activities that involved the validation of items. The first had to do with item quality and content alignment. A team of trained raters, trained by personnel from the University of Wisconsin Educational Research Center and directed by Gatti Evaluation, looked at each item on the Unit and End-of-Year Benchmark Tests to verify that the item is of the highest quality and aligns in content with the state curriculum standards of major states.

The second was the empirical field-testing or "validation" of key assessment components in a classroom setting in schools chosen to be representative of the nation's school population. Rather than conducting these tryouts prior to program publication in an unrealistic situation in which the corresponding instructional program was not used, Scott Foresman management made the critical decision to validate the tests as used during the course of their implementation in an actual instructional program. The decision was also made to include excess test material—reading and listening passages and individual test items—in the validation version of these assessments. This permitted BETA psychometric staff and Scott Foresman editorial personnel to select the best-performing subset of items for inclusion in the final versions of the tests. This is a technically superior way of validating tests, rather then revising test items based on field-test data and hoping that the revised versions will be superior to the earlier ones. Such a tryout design also improves the validity of the resulting instruments, as the data collection takes place at the intended point in the school year at which the instruments are to be used. For example, each unit of the Benchmark Tests was piloted immediately following instruction in the assessed content. While this design obviously requires an entire school year for implementation, the resulting assessment components are empirically validated.

How will your program help prepare my students for required state and other standardized tests?

In many ways! The Student Editions, Teacher's Editions, and Practice Books are all carefully crafted to teach the knowledge, skills, and strategies the children need to succeed in all their reading and writing tasks. Many Practice Book pages contain items that reflect common standardized test formats, allowing children repeated opportunities to become familiar with question patterns. In addition, the Weekly Selection Tests and the Unit Benchmark Tests are similarly constructed to provide further practice. Tips on instructional strategies designed to prepare your children for high-stakes tests are described in Chapter 2 of this handbook and in Chapter 4, where they are tailored for English language learners. With the preparation provided by Scott Foresman materials, your students will be ready to face any test-taking situation.

How do I find out where my students are at the beginning of the year?

Finding a starting point for each student can be difficult. Scott Foresman makes it easier by providing test options and parent and learner surveys to help you get to know your students.

Group-administered Baseline Tests give you information about the instructional needs of your class and point you to program features that meet those needs. Student Surveys familiarize you with each student's reading attitudes and interests, while Parent Surveys give you insights into their literacy habits and behaviors when they are not in school. All of these sources of assessment information work together to help you find a starting point for each child in your class.

How do I know that my students are being tested on the right skills?

Scott Foresman Reading Street is founded on a carefully crafted scope and sequence of skills, based on the most current research and accepted practices in reading instruction, and systematically aligned with national and state language arts and reading standards.

This scope and sequence is the basis for both the instructional plan and for the depth and breadth of the Scott Foresman Assessment Program. Target skills and strategies are taught in every lesson and then assessed in the Weekly Selection Test. Each target skill is also assessed in the Unit Benchmark Test after it has been taught three times. This systematic coordination of instruction and assessment ensures that students are being tested on *what* they are being taught—in the way they are being taught.

What is the best way to assess my students? How does your program provide what I need?

Accurate and ongoing assessment enables teachers to check student's achievement and growth, to evaluate classroom instruction, and to help children monitor their own learning. An effective assessment system incorporates a variety of assessment methods—both formal and informal—to help teachers meet those varied purposes.

Scott Foresman provides a full complement of materials to meet your assessment requirements. For a formal assessment of unit skills and selections, you'll find several different tests from which to choose. For informal Assessment, the *Assessment Handbook* contains surveys, observation forms, and reporting forms in English and Spanish, as well as questioning and observation techniques you can adapt for your classroom needs. The informal strategies will assist you in making student self-assessment, peer assessment, portfolios, and grading more efficient. Chapters 2 and 3 of the *Assessment Handbook* describe all of the formal and informal assessments. Also, the Teacher's Edition provides tools for you to make both immediate and long-term decisions about the instructional needs of your students.

How does your program support assessment of my English language learners?

Scott Foresman recognizes the unique challenges and rewards of teaching and assessing the progress of English language learners. Chapter 4 of the *Assessment Handbook* discusses research-based methods of assessing the strengths and needs of English language learners in your classroom. Scott Foresman formal and informal classroom-based assessments reflect those methods as they help teachers monitor growth in the basic reading and expression skills of alphabetic understanding, decoding, sight vocabulary, and grammar, along with measurement of the more complex skills of fluency, comprehension, and vocabulary. The chapter provides guidance on instructional strategies designed to prepare English language learners for formal assessments, including high-stakes tests, as well as advice on appropriate use of accommodations for Scott Foresman formal assessments.

Will your program help me when I have to assign grades?

Because we know that grading is a major concern for many teachers, the *Assessment Handbook* contains an entire chapter devoted to grading. You will find guidance on record keeping, designing scoring rubrics, grading student participation in class discussions and group activities, grading oral presentations, and assessing individual or group writing. The chapter also offers a general discussion of purposes, recommendations, and issues related to grading. Add to this the many formal testing opportunities, which are an integral part of the program, and you have an assessment program that gives you the information you need to meet your assessment requirements.

Program Assessment Overview

A variety of assessment instruments, used with fictional and nonfictional selections, allow you to

- determine students' strengths and needs
- monitor students' progress
- measure students' skill and strategy proficiencies
- evaluate the effectiveness of instruction from the beginning of the year to the end!

Baseline Group Tests

Weekly Selection Tests

Fresh Reads for Differentiated Test Practice

Unit Benchmark Tests

End-of-Year Benchmark Tests

Assessment Handbooks

Technology

Beginning of the Year
Diagnose and Differentiate/Establish Baseline Data

Baseline Group Test

- Is administered as a placement test to your entire class
- Provides options for group and individual administration
- Identifies your below-level students requiring strategic intervention
- Identifies your on-level students
- Identifies your above-level students requiring challenge
- Helps you use *Scott Foresman Reading Street* features and components to focus instruction on students' needs
- Establishes baseline data

Assessment Handbook for Grades 3–6

Informal classroom-based assessment strategies and tools, including:

- Student and Parent Surveys
- Reading, writing, and oral-language Teacher Checklists
- Running Records
- Teacher Observation
- Portfolios

During the Year
Monitor Progress/Assess and Regroup

Teacher's Editions

- Ongoing Assessment
- Monitor Progress Boxes
- Student Self-Monitoring
- Guiding Comprehension Questions
- Reading Fluency Assessment
- Reader Response Questions
- Practice for Standardized Tests
- Retelling Scoring Rubrics
- Writing Scoring Rubrics
- Spelling Tests

Practice Book

- Practice pages in standardized test
- Practice skills sure to be on tests
- Helps you identify students needing more instruction

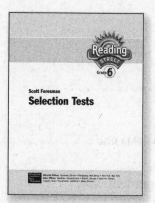

Weekly Selection Tests

- Are administered mid-week
- Contain vocabulary and comprehension sections
- Measure "target" and "review" comprehension skills in the context of authentic literature
- Combine multiple-choice and constructed-response questions about the weekly selections

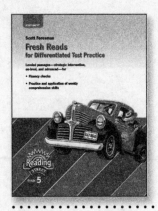

Fresh Reads for Differentiated Test Practice

- Are administered weekly
- Provide a leveled reading selection for below-level, on-level, and advanced-level students
- Give students opportunities to practice the "target" and "review" comprehension skills each week
- Combine multiple-choice and constructed-response questions about the selection

Unit Benchmark Tests

- Are administered at the end of each unit
- Provide one or two new reading selections
- Assess unit "target" and "review" comprehension skills, vocabulary strategies, high-frequency words, and phonics skills, as well as grammar, usage, mechanics skills, and writing
- Combine multiple-choice and constructed-response questions
- Provide an integrated approach to assessment

Assessment Handbook for Grades 3–6

Informal classroom-based assessment strategies and tools, including:

- Grading guidance
- Ongoing teacher observation
- Running records
- Anecdotal records
- Retellings and rubrics
- Teacher-Student Conference Record form
- Reading and Writing Strategy Assessment forms
- Peer Assessment form
- Portfolio logs
- Summary forms

Technology

- Fluency Coach: Oral reading fluency assessment (WCPM) and practice
- Success Tracker: Online assessment and data management with diagnostic prescriptions and alignment to standards
- Exam View: Test generator with alignment to state standards and prescriptions

End of the Year
Administer Summative Assessment

End-of-Year Benchmark Test

- Is a cumulative test administered at the end of each grade
- Provides three reading selections
- Tests "target" and "review" comprehension skills, vocabulary strategies, high-frequency words, and phonics skills, as well as grammar, usage, mechanics skills, and writing
- Combines multiple-choice and constructed-response questions
- Provides an integrated approach to assessment

Assessment Handbook for Grades 3–6

Informal classroom-based assessment strategies and tools, including:
- Grading guidance
- Teacher-Student Conference Record form
- Reading and Writing Strategy Assessment forms
- Summary forms

Technology

- Fluency Coach: Oral reading fluency assessment (WCPM) and practice
- Success Tracker: Online assessment and data management with diagnostic prescriptions and alignment to standards
- Exam View: Test generator with alignment to state standards and prescriptions

 # Assessment Literacy

Classroom teachers make an extraordinary number of decisions every hour of the school day. Four important decisions are:

1. What are the critical understandings and skills that I want the students to know and be able to do upon completion of this lesson/unit/grade?

2. How will I know if the students have accomplished this?

3. What will I do to support those who have not?

4. What will I do to support those who already have?

The critical understandings and skills are the **learning targets,** usually based on school, district, and/or state curriculum standards. The second question is the focus of this introductory section of the handbook. ***How will I know? What evidence must I collect?***

While Scott Foresman offers many valuable resources, strategies, and tools for collecting evidence of achievement, educators must be wise about the subject of **assessment**—what it is, when to use it, how to do it, and why it is so important.

What Is Assessment Literacy?

Now, more than ever before, it is important for all teachers and administrators to be "literate" about educational assessment and evaluation. Why? Research tells us that the use of meaningful classroom assessment strategies and tools, such as questioning, observational methods, and student self-assessment, empowers educators, guides instruction, and improves learning.

Further, we cannot ignore that increased demands for accountability at the state and national levels, including Reading First, No Child Left Behind (NCLB), and Adequate Yearly Progress (AYP), have produced an unprecedented proliferation of testing. Students' test performance has become the accountability yardstick by which the effectiveness of schools, districts, states, and even teaching is measured and judged.

To be informed consumers and creators of assessment, individuals must:

• Understand the power of assessment in promoting student achievement

• Become knowledgeable about the functions, strengths, and limitations of formal and informal assessment

• Maintain a balance of summative and formative assessments in their classrooms and schools

• Embrace standards of quality as they evaluate and create assessments

• Use sound assessment practices to design and administer quality classroom-based assessments

What Is Assessment?

The Latin root of the word "assess" means "to sit beside." This is a much gentler notion of this concept than most of us have, although "sitting beside" students to confer about the development of a story in progress, to conduct a running record, or to observe a group discussion are valuable assessment techniques.

Assessment is simply the gathering and interpretation of evidence about student learning. There are many methods for collecting information to determine if students have mastered the knowledge and skills, or the learning targets. We can use a variety of formal and informal measures to collect that evidence.

Formal and Informal Measures

Formal assessment measures are most often regarded as tests—tasks presented to students in order to obtain systematic evidence about their performance. The tasks are designed to provide samples of individual achievement and are administered, scored, and interpreted according to prescribed conditions.

Often, formal assessments are regarded as **summative** because they come at the end of an instructional process and are used to determine placement or assign grades. Examples are chapter tests, unit projects, and final examinations. (Airasian, 2000)

Standardized tests are formal assessments designed to be administered to large numbers of test takers. Testing conditions, such as precise directions, time allowances, and security procedures, are tightly controlled. The tests are administered at the same time each year. Test questions are written, reviewed, and revised following tryouts by a representative sample of the population for which the instrument is designed.

Examples of standardized tests are commercially published tests, as well as state assessments, which are now used annually to measure student achievement of standards for reporting and accountability purposes, in compliance with federal NCLB legislation and other mandates. These tests are often called "high-stakes," because scores are made very public, and schools and districts are subject to sanctions and embarrassment if they do not make annual AYP goals. (Popham, 2004)

Informal Assessment: Dr. Richard Stiggins distinguishes between assessment *of* learning and assessment *for* learning. Assessments *of* learning are generally formal assessments administered at the end of an instructional period. They answer the question, "How much have students learned as of a particular point in time?" (Stiggins, 2002)

Informal assessment is classroom-based assessment *for* learning that helps us *dig deeper* in order to ascertain exactly *how* individual students are making progress toward achievement of the learning targets.

While these assessment tasks may not be the same type or depth for all students, and may not be recorded in a prescribed, standardized manner, they are not "informal" in the sense of "casual" or "random." Instead, informal assessment is thoughtfully planned and intentional monitoring of learning that takes place *during* the instructional process, rather than the evaluation of learning at the conclusion of the process.

Examples of informal assessments are teachers' questions, observations, homework, quizzes, and individual conferences with students. These assessments are often called **formative** assessments, because they are influential in "forming" the process under way and are intended to guide and inform instruction.

Balancing Formative and Summative Assessment

Annually administered tests, such as state assessments, provide general feedback about students' performance related to broad content standards, or achievement targets. These tests are not designed to offer the immediate and ongoing information about achievement that teachers need to make critical instructional decisions. Even once-a-unit classroom tests do not provide sufficient information to improve teaching and increase learning. (Stiggins, 2004)

> "Balance continuous classroom assessment in support of learning with periodic assessments verifying learning."
> (Stiggins 2002)

To establish and maintain productive, learning-centered classroom environments, teachers rely on a balance of informal assessments *for* learning and formal assessments *of* learning to guide their instruction. They use an array of formative and summative measures *derived from* and/or *aligned with* the curriculum content standards and objectives and based on their assessment purposes.

Why and when do we use formative assessment?

- To diagnose students' strengths and needs

- To elicit prior knowledge for a concept or topic

- To provide frequent feedback to students that is descriptive and helpful, rather than judgmental, as in grades

- To motivate learners to increase effort as they experience incremental successes

- To build students' confidence in themselves as learners

- To help students take responsibility for their learning as they monitor their progress and adjust their goals

- To plan, modify, and regulate the pace of instruction to meet the needs of all students

- To communicate with parents and caregivers (e.g., learning expectations, students' progress in meeting learning targets, and methods of providing support at home)

Why and when do we use summative assessment?

- To report achievement of content standards, the learning targets

- To document growth over time (e.g., unit-to-unit, year-to-year)

- To assign grades appropriately at the end of a unit or for a report card, for instance

- To validate judgments and decisions about student achievement

- To recommend students for promotion and placement in special programs

- To gauge program effectiveness, note strengths, and identify gaps

- To examine comparative data across schools and districts in order to make programmatic decisions (e.g., establish school-improvement priorities, improve curriculum alignment, or establish the need for intervention programs or additional resources)

- To satisfy state and federal accountability mandates, such as AYP

- To inform the public (e.g., tax payers, business leaders, legislators)

Evaluating Assessments for Quality

Most textbooks and instructional programs, including *Scott Foresman Reading Street,* have accompanying assessments for teachers to use. The formal and informal measures within *Scott Foresman Reading Street* reflect the highest standards of quality and seamlessly align with the instructional program. Teachers may also wish occasionally to construct their own tests and performance assessments for other content areas and interdisciplinary studies.

> "...The current model of standards-based reform, so prevalent in the discourse of national and state efforts, positions content standards as the primary driving force behind just about every other educational phenomenon."
> (Pearson 2001)

In order to implement fair and sound assessment, teachers are encouraged to consider the following standards for evaluating the quality of commercial assessments and for designing their own classroom assessments to augment or replace the textbook measures.

Know Your Learning Targets

Statewide and district-wide curriculum statements embody the content knowledge and skills we want our students to have, and they are the basis for all our testing. They may be labeled as content standards, benchmarks, learning objectives, expectations, or goals. The main point is *know* what the learning targets are, and teach them to the students.

- "Unpack" the content standards to identify the underlying knowledge, concepts, processes, skills, and dispositions (that is to say, attitudes, values, or habits of mind) that become the **learning targets.**

- Translate the targets into student-friendly language.

- Post the targets in the classroom for all to see.

- Discuss the targets with the students at the beginning of the instructional process (e.g., lesson, unit, marking period).

- Review them throughout the process so that students have clear, reachable targets to hit.

Determine the Match

Teachers must carefully scrutinize each test item to ensure that the assessment has **content validity.** To what extent does the assessment measure what it is being used to measure? Does the content of the test or task represent a balanced and adequate sampling of the targeted knowledge and skills as they are taught in the classroom? In other words, a recall exercise in which students are to match vocabulary words with their definitions would not be a valid assessment of a vocabulary standard requiring students to use structural analysis and context clues to determine word meanings. Test questions and tasks should clearly reflect the learning targets and require students to perform the behaviors as you have taught them.

Consider the Amount

An effective assessment measures only a modest number of important learning targets, and measures them well, so that teachers and students are not overwhelmed by the length and complexity of the activity. (Popham, 2004) Assessments are meant to sample components of the learning taking place in the classroom, so an appropriate test or task must also contain a sufficient number of items related to each sampled learning target. In this way, teachers can be confident that the results will identify target skill areas that have been thoroughly taught and those that need improvement.

Strive for Reliability and Fairness

Reliability: How trustworthy is this assessment? Can I rely on the scores? Will this assessment give me the same results about the same learning targets every time?

Scoring of selected-response tests is considered quite reliable, and two teachers scoring the same set of multiple-choice tests will probably get the same results, barring a small chance of human error.

Although constructed-response assessments may measure more meaningful learning targets, they are considered less reliable because scoring is based on judgment.

To increase reliability, many states and school districts develop scoring rubrics and train scorers in a thorough, systematic way. Panels of raters score a large number of papers and discuss their scores until they're consistent in their ratings. Some papers are chosen as anchor papers because the raters believe they exemplify score points on the rubric. These papers are then used to guide subsequent scoring sessions, and reliability is improved.

This activity can be replicated at the building level as teachers of the same grade level collaborate to design and score performance assessments, such as end-of-unit projects and presentations.

Fairness: Do all students, including those with diverse cultural and linguistic backgrounds, have an equal chance to demonstrate what they know and can do? Have all of them had the same opportunity to learn the content? Are the directions clear? Is the environment comfortable?

Fairness in assessment is compromised when teachers assess knowledge and skills that have not been taught or use assessment formats that do not reflect how the learning targets have been taught (e.g., asking for opinions and reasons when the emphasis has been on recall of facts).

Designing Quality Classroom Assessments

Teachers can construct multi-purpose classroom assessments that reflect these standards of quality—validity, reliability, and fairness. Purposes include diagnosing students' strengths and needs; planning, monitoring, and adjusting instruction; and providing feedback to students, parents, and others regarding progress and proficiency. The following design questions are intended to guide educators as they plan and build their own assessments:

1. **What learning target(s) will you assess?**

2. **For which formative or summative purpose(s) is this assessment being administered?**

   - To detect strengths and needs
   - To motivate learners
   - To assign grades
   - To check progress
   - To group for instruction
   - To collect additional evidence
   - To evaluate instruction
   - Other

3. **Who will use the results of this assessment?**

   - Students
   - Teacher(s)
   - Parent
   - Principal
   - Community
   - Other

4. What format will the assessment take?

It is important to select the format that most appropriately matches the target. For example, you wouldn't create a multiple-choice test to assess students' *use* of action verbs in their writing. Rather, you would assign a constructed-response activity asking them to incorporate action verbs in their text.

Conversely, you wouldn't use constructed-response format to assess students' identification of states and their capitals. An activity requiring them to match states and capitals would suffice for this purpose—assessing recall. Constructed responses are valuable because they help us seek insights into students' reasoning behind their answers or evidence that they can apply what they have learned. Possible assessment formats and examples of activities are listed in the table at the end of this topic.

5. What criteria will you use to evaluate performance?

- How will you know it when you see it?

- What does hitting the target look like? What are the qualities?

- Is there one right answer or several possible answers?

- What will you accept as evidence that students have hit the target, that is, that they have acquired the knowledge and skills identified in the content standards?

6. What type of feedback will be provided to guide improvement?

How will results be communicated? How will you tell the story behind the numbers? Will you use a letter grade, a rubric score, written descriptive comments, a checklist, a point on a continuum of learning, such as an oral language behaviors' continuum, or another way?

The most valuable feedback is very specific and descriptive of how the performance hits (or does not hit) the target. Give concrete suggestions rather than vague comments or encouragement, such as "Nice work!" or "You can do better next time!" Share clear examples of successful work with the students, and have them compare their work with the model. Allow students opportunities to revise their performances.

Transforming learning expectations into assessment tasks, assigning criteria, designing scoring procedures, and preparing feedback are challenging and time-consuming activities when they are attempted alone.

It is a rewarding and collegial experience to collaborate with peers in articulating expectations, designing common assessments, analyzing student work, and selecting anchor/model performances. When educators work together to become assessment literate, they empower each other with the ability to improve assessment practices and accountability systems in their school districts and states. More importantly, they increase learning for students.

Assessment Design Options

Possible Format	Examples of Tasks	Suggested Scoring/Feedback
Selected Response	• Multiple choice • Matching • True-false	One right answer; cut scores and percentages
Short Constructed Response (written/oral)	• Fill in the blank • Sentence completion • Graphic organizer • Brief response to prompt	One (or few) right answers; cut scores and percentages
Extended Constructed Response (written/oral)	• Prompt-based narrative, descriptive, expository, and persuasive writing • Retellings • Position with support • Summaries	More than one right answer; scoring with checklists, descriptive criteria, standards; continuum, rubrics, comparative models
Performances	• Oral presentation • Demonstration • Discussion • Role play	More than one right answer; scoring with checklists, descriptive criteria, standards, continuum, rubrics, peer and self-evaluation; comparative models
Products	• Science project • Visual display • Model • Video • Poem, story, play • Log/journal • Portfolio	More than one right answer; scoring with checklists, descriptive criteria, standards, continuum, rubrics, comparative models
Processes	• Strategy applications (e.g., think-alouds, questioning) • Teacher-student conferences • Peer and group assessments • Student self-assessments • Interviews • Inventories • Observations • Book club participation • Surveys of reading or writing behaviors • Portfolio entry slips • Response logs • Reading/writing lists	No right answer; do not score; collect as additional evidence; provide descriptive feedback to students

What is the *Scott Foresman Reading Street* Assessment System?

All assessments in the program reflect current theories of teaching language and literacy, and are aligned with solid classroom teaching practices.

Scott Foresman Reading Street offers a seamless assessment cycle at each grade. The formal and informal assessments, combined with assessable moments during instruction, become a continuous cycle where one is always informing the other, resulting in a seamless learning program for the students.

Fundamental to the cycle are clear, grade-appropriate, and important learning targets that are aligned with national and state curriculum content standards.

> To prepare students for standardized tests, teachers should teach "the key ideas and processes contained in content standards in rich and engaging ways; by collecting evidence of student understanding of that content through robust local assessments, rather than one-shot standardized testing; and by using engaging and effective instructional strategies that help students explore core concepts through inquiry and problem solving."
>
> (McTighe, Seif, & Wiggins 2004)

- At each grade the cycle begins with the administration of a baseline assessment to establish a starting point for placing students and to determine the amount of instructional support they will need in order to hit the targets. The use of DIBELS (Dynamic Indicators of Basic Early Literacy Skills) allows teachers to diagnose students' specific needs in reading, such as accuracy, fluency, and vocabulary.

- Progress is then monitored daily and weekly through informal assessments, such as teacher observations, running records, retellings, and conferencing, as well as formal assessments.

- The Weekly Selection Tests assess students' understanding of the weekly reading selections, and the Fresh Reads for Differentiated Test Practice give students opportunities to practice comprehension and build fluency with new selections matched to their instructional levels.

- The Unit Benchmark Tests and the End-of-Year Benchmark Tests are summative assessments designed to assess students' understanding of the targeted skills, strategies, and critical thinking skills taught throughout the unit and the school year.

What are the assessment targets?

Reading

What are the reading targets? The National Reading Panel was convened to assess the research-based knowledge and effectiveness of various methods of teaching reading. In their 2000 report, the panelists concluded that certain reading skills take priority over others and are essential as students learn to become independent, strategic readers and writers.

Scott Foresman Reading Street emphasizes the **priority skills** that are proven to be indicators of reading success:

Phonemic awareness is the ability to identify the separate sounds, or *phonemes*, that make up spoken words, and to alter and arrange sounds to create new words. It is a subset of phonological awareness, a broad term meaning the awareness of sounds in spoken language. Knowledge of phonemic awareness allows students to hear separate sounds, recognize a sound's position in a word, manipulate sounds, and understand the role sounds play in language. In *Scott Foresman Reading Street,* phonemic awareness instructional and assessment activities include isolating, blending, segmenting, deleting, adding, and substituting phonemes.

Phonics is the study of how letters represent sounds in *written* language, unlike phonemic awareness, which is strictly *oral*. Phonics instruction and assessment in *Scott Foresman Reading Street* include:

- **Print awareness**—Understanding the relationship between oral and written language, that written language carries meaning, and that print is read from left to right

- **Alphabetic knowledge**—Knowledge of the shapes, names, and sounds of letters

- **Alphabetic principle**—Understanding that there is a systematic relationship between sounds (phonemes) and letters (graphemes)

- **Decoding**—The process of analyzing letter-sound patterns in words to ascertain meaning

- **Knowledge of high-frequency words**—Sometimes called "sight words," these are the words that appear most often in our written language. Because students need to know these words when they read stories and write sentences, these words are introduced before students have learned many letter-sound patterns. Many high-frequency words cannot be decoded easily because of irregular and uncommon letter-sound patterns. Others do conform to phonics rules but must be taught as whole words because students have not yet learned the letter-sound relationships within them.

Fluency is the ability to effortlessly, quickly, and accurately decode letters, words, sentences, and passages. Fluent readers are able to group words into meaningful grammatical units and read with proper expression. Fluency is an essential component of comprehension and is assessed regularly in *Scott Foresman Reading Street.*

> "Priority skills are those instructional goals that are the best predictors of reading success for students at an identified time in their reading growth."
> (Vaughn & Linan-Thompson 2004)

Vocabulary acquisition and development contribute significantly to overall text comprehension. While extensive reading experiences with varied text types and opportunities for classroom discussion are known to increase word knowledge, *Scott Foresman Reading Street* explicitly teaches and assesses vocabulary skills through the study of context clues, word structure, and dictionary/glossary use.

- Context clues from the words or phrases surrounding an unknown word help readers identify its meaning. Context clues include synonyms, antonyms, definitions, explanations, descriptions, and examples that appear within the text surrounding an unfamiliar word.

- The study of word structure is the analysis of word-meaning elements to make meaning of the word as a whole. Such meaningful elements include word roots, prefixes, suffixes, and compound words. Syllabication generalizations and inflected endings, which change the tense, case, or singular-plural form of words, but do not affect meaning or part of speech, are also taught and assessed.

> "Having a strong vocabulary is not only a school goal, it is a characteristic that allows us to participate actively in our world, and it is viewed by those we meet as the hallmark of an educated person."
> (Blachowicz 2005)

- Understanding what dictionaries/glossaries are and why, when, and how to use them helps to increase students vocabularies. Students become familiar with the organization and format of dictionaries and glossaries and are guided and assessed in their use of the components of an entry, including syllabication, pronunciation, part of speech, etymology, and definition.

Text comprehension, the overarching goal of reading, is the active process of constructing meaning from text. It is a complex process in which readers apply their prior knowledge and experiences, use their understandings about text (types, structures, features, etc.), and intentionally employ an array of before-, during-, and after-reading strategies and skills in order to attain meaning. Effective readers combine their own experiences with their interpretation of the author's intent as they work to make sense of ideas in text.

In *Scott Foresman Reading Street,* students' use of targeted comprehension strategies and skills is monitored continuously on the Weekly Selection Tests and Fresh Reads for Differentiated Test Practice. Students in grades 3–6 read a variety of engaging narrative and expository texts and respond to appropriate multiple-choice and constructed-response questions designed to assess how they use the comprehension skills in constructing meaning. There are three types of comprehension questions that correspond to the *In the Book* and *In My Head* categories of questions in the instructional program.

Literal questions, which focus on ideas explicitly stated in the text, although *not necessarily* verbatim. In response to these items, students *recognize* and *identify* information that might be found in a single sentence or in two or more sentences of contiguous text.

Inferential questions, which are based on the theme, key concepts, and major ideas of the passage and often require students to *interpret* information from across parts of the text and to *connect* knowledge from the text with their own general background knowledge.

Critical-analysis questions, which are also inferential in nature and focus on important ideas in the selection. Yet, they differ from inferential questions in that readers are required to stand apart from the text and *analyze, synthesize,* and/or *evaluate* the quality, effectiveness, relevance, and consistency of the message, rhetorical features (tone, style, voice, etc.), author or character motivation, and the author's purpose or credibility.

Throughout the program, students are scaffolded and guided as they move from literal understanding, to inferential comprehension, to critical analysis of text.

Writing

Skills include:

- Elaborating on ideas
- Focusing on main idea/topic
- Writing with a personal interest
- Connecting ideas with appropriate order words
- Selecting precise words
- Constructing sentences of various lengths and types
- Controlling mechanical aspects of writing

FORMAL ASSESSMENTS

The **Unit Benchmark Tests** and **End-of-Year Benchmark Tests** require responses to narrative, descriptive, expository, and persuasive writing prompts. The Writing Scoring Rubrics assess six traits:

- Focus/Ideas
- Organization/Paragraphs
- Voice
- Word choice
- Sentences
- Conventions

- **Myself as a Reader and Writer** is a questionanaire in which students reflect on their own reading and writing habits at the beginning of the school year.

- Written **Retellings** demonstrate students' ability to understand narrative and expository text elements and to recall and record information in writing.

- **Writing Logs** allow students to monitor their writing growth over time.

- **About My Writing** is a form in which students reflect on their writing progress at various points during the school year.

- **Writing Strategy Assessments** help teachers synthesize information about students' writing progress and use of writing strategies.

- **Teacher-Student Conferences** provide insights about students' writing behaviors and strategies.

- **Student Portfolios**, containing draft and final copies of work, give evidence of students' growth and progress in writing.

Grammar, Usage, and Mechanics

Skills include:

- Sentences

- Parts of speech, i.e., nouns, verbs, adjectives, adverbs, pronouns (contractions), prepositions, conjunctions, and interjections

- Capitalization, punctuation, and indentation

Skills are assessed through the formal assessments, **Unit Benchmark Tests** and **End-of-Year Benchmark Tests**. The Writing Scoring Rubrics assess sentence structure, fluency, and variety, as well as control of writing conventions.

Speaking and Listening

Skills include:

- Preparing to speak to a group

- Speaking with appropriate purposes

- Speaking with an appropriate delivery and manner

- Listening with appropriate purposes

- Evaluating a speaker's delivery and message

Informal assessments that allow you to document students' oral language development throughout the year include oral **Retellings, Teacher-Student Conference Records, Ongoing Teacher Observation,** and **Student Portfolios. Student Self-Assessments** are opportunities for students to monitor and evaluate their growth in speaking and listening and to set goals for improvement.

Research/Study Skills

Skills include:

- Understanding and using graphic sources, such as charts, maps, diagrams, graphs, and so on.

- Understanding and using reference sources, such as dictionaries, encyclopedias, library databases, and so on.

- Understanding and using the research process.

Skills are assessed informally by having students demonstrate the ability to perform a task involving the use of the skill.

References

Airasian, P. W. *Classroom Assessment: Concepts and Applications.* McGraw-Hill, 2000.

Blachowicz, C. L. Z. "Vocabulary Essentials: From Research to Practice for Improved Instruction." *Research-Based Vocabulary Instruction.* Scott Foresman, forthcoming.

McTighe, J., Seif, E., and Wiggins, G. "You Can Teach for Meaning." *Educational Leadership*, 62 (1), (September 2004), pp. 26–30.

National Reading Panel. "Teaching Children to Read: An Evidence-Based Assessment of the Scientific Research Literature on Reading and Its Implications for Reading Instruction." *Reports of the Subgroups.* National Institute for Literacy, National Institute of Child Health and Human Development, 2000.

Pearson, P. D. "Learning to Teach Reading: The Status of the Knowledge Base." *Learning to Teach Reading: Setting the Research Agenda.* Roller, C. M., ed., pp. 4–19. International Reading Association, 2001.

Popham, W. J. "Tawdry Tests and AYP." *Educational Leadership,* 62 (2), (October 2004), pp. 85–86.

Stiggins, R. J. "Assessment Crisis: The Absence of Assessment for Learning." *Kappan Professional Journal.* http://www.pdkintl.org/kappan/k020sti.htm (accessed May 8, 2005).

Stiggins, R. "New Assessment Beliefs for a New School Mission." *Phi Delta Kappan,* 86 (1), (September 2004), pp. 22–27.

Vaughn, S., & Linan-Thompson, S. *Research-Based Methods of Reading Instruction. Grades K–3.* Association for Supervision and Curriculum Development, 2004.

Chapter 2 # Formal (Summative) Assessment of Learning

Overview

What is formal, or summative, assessment?

- A systematic method of gathering information about students' knowledge and skills typically based on written tests, each designed for a specific purpose

- Tests designed to provide a sample of individual performance, administered, scored, and interpreted according to prescribed directions.

- In *Scott Foresman Reading Street*, a means of determining students' progress at various checkpoints throughout the school year

Why should we use formal assessments?

- Continuous assessment and evaluation are critical to successful teaching and learning.

- Gathering information in a systematic way can be used to validate judgments and decisions about learning.

- Formal assessments provide the same opportunity for each student taking the test.

  - Each student receives the same directions.

  - Each test is scored by the same criteria.

- Feedback from formal assessments enables students to learn about their own literacy development.

- The system of formal assessments supported and enhanced with classroom-based assessments in *Scott Foresman Reading Street* helps teachers to continually refine and modify instruction in the classroom to meet the needs of the students.

> "Tests should be considered nothing more than attempts to systematically gather information. The bottom line in selecting and using any assessment should be whether it helps students."
>
> (Farr 1992)

How does using both formal and informal assessment benefit my students?

- Assessment occurs continuously throughout the day every day in every teacher's classroom. When you ask questions or when you observe students working on an assignment, you are conducting classroom-based assessments.

- The knowledge gained from using both these forms of assessment together will provide you with a comprehensive picture of your students' skills and abilities.

- Both are quite important, and, when used together, they form a solid basis for making educationally sound decisions for students.

What options are available?

Scott Foresman Reading Street includes a series of formal assessments with differing purposes that provide a range of information about students' proficiency.

What kinds of formal assessments are included in this program?

- Baseline Group Tests (3–6)
- DIBELS (3–6) (optional)
- Weekly Selection Tests (3–6)
- Fresh Reads for Differentiated Test Practice (3–6)
- Unit Benchmark Tests (3–6)
- End-of-Year Benchmark Tests (3–6)

What are the functions of the different kinds of tests?

- Use **Baseline Group Tests** when you need to establish baseline data for determining the level of instructional support students need and placing them into instructional groups.

- Use **DIBELS (Dynamic Indicators of Basic Early Literacy Skills)** to show students' mastery of very specific skills proven to be indicators of reading success.

- Use **Weekly Selection Tests** when you want to assess students' understanding of the content and vocabulary of main selections.

- Use **Fresh Reads for Differentiated Test Practice** to give students an opportunity to practice comprehension skills with a selection matched to each student's instructional level.

- Use **Unit Benchmark Tests** to assess students' understanding of skills, strategies, and critical thinking skills taught throughout the unit.

- Use the **End-of-Year Benchmark Tests** to assess students' understanding of skills, strategies, and critical thinking skills taught throughout the year.

Why are there so many different types of tests to administer?

- Reading is complex, involving interactions among reader, text, and context; use of multiple measures provides an accurate and complete picture of the students.

- By having a variety of assessments, you can select the ones that will be most useful for you and the students.

> "No single instrument or technique can adequately measure achievement in reading..."
> (Winograd 1993)

© Pearson Education

Do I have to use all the formal assessments?

Select the tests that meet the assessment needs of your students and align best with your curriculum and instruction.

What instructional strategies will help to prepare the students for formal assessments and high-stakes tests?

- Use the *Scott Foresman Reading Street* program to continually monitor students' progress and refine instruction to reflect their needs.

- Use the administration of the formal assessments as a way to teach test-taking skills.

- Literal, inferential, and critical-analysis questions on the formal assessments are based on the question-answer framework used in instruction and are similar to question types on high-stakes assessments.

- Daily practice in answering, analyzing, and asking Right There, Think and Search, and Author and Me questions will improve students' achievement on high-stakes standardized tests.

- Download and examine released forms of state and standardized assessments, reviewing the various item constructions and test vocabulary. Model and discuss the thinking steps involved in responding to both multiple-choice and constructed-response items.

- Pre-teach the "language of tests" encountered in directions and test items, including

  - Question words: *who, what, which, where, when, why,* and *how*

  - Emphasis words: *not, except, most likely, probably, main, both, neither, either, most,* and *least*

  - Action words: *tell, answer, mark, describe,* and *support with evidence*

- Encourage the students to be careful readers and to check their own work.

- Provide repeated opportunities for practicing all the techniques above.

References

Farr, R. "Putting It All Together: Solving the Reading Assessment Problem." *The Reading Teacher,* 46, 1992, pp. 26–37. Reprinted in *Reading Assessment in Practice* (International Reading Association, 1995).

Winograd, P., Paris, S., and Bridge, C. "Improving the Assessment of Literacy." *The Reading Teacher,* 45, 1992, pp. 108–116. Reprinted in *Reading Assessment in Practice* (International Reading Association, 1995).

Baseline Group Test

What is it?
- A placement test given at the beginning of the school year to establish a baseline for each student

Why would I choose it?
- To identify students who are on grade level, those who need intervention, and those who could benefit from more challenge
- To recognize how best to shape the curriculum to fit the needs of all students

What does it test?
- In Grade 3, phonics, vocabulary words, reading-comprehension skills, and phonemic awareness are tested. Also included are a graded oral vocabulary test and a passage for testing fluency and/or doing a running record (both optional).
- In grades 4–6, vocabulary words and reading-comprehension skills are tested. Also included are a graded oral vocabulary test and a passage for testing fluency and/or doing a running record (both optional).

When do I use it?
- At the beginning of the school year, to establish baselines for students and to place them in groups according to their level of ability
- Throughout the year as needed to assess progress and determine instructional requirements of new students

How do I use it?
- The test is designed to be group administered
- Each test includes a table specifying how many correct responses indicate the various levels of mastery (Strategic Intervention, On-Level, or Advanced)

How do I use the results?
- The teacher manual includes charts with percentage scores, an evaluation chart, and an interpretation key that will allow you to place each student in an appropriate instructional group

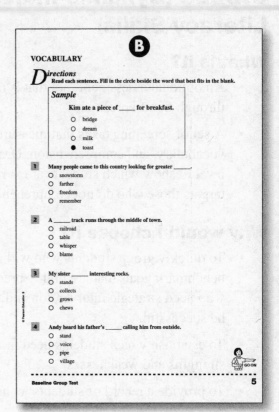

PHONICS

Directions
Read each word. Fill in the circle beside the word that has the same sound as the underlined letter or letters.

Sample
cup
○ sun   ● like   ○ push   ○ chin

1 <u>wr</u>ite
○ wait   ○ room   ○ cow   ○ date

2 c<u>oi</u>n
○ draw   ○ boy   ○ care   ○ pond

3 sh<u>ou</u>t
○ how   ○ boat   ○ true   ○ does

4 tr<u>ea</u>t
○ her   ○ head   ○ keep   ○ men

5 s<u>a</u>me
○ back   ○ name   ○ can   ○ face

© Pearson Education 3

Baseline Group Test   **3**

VOCABULARY

Directions
Read each sentence. Fill in the circle beside the word that best fits in the blank.

Sample
Kim ate a piece of _____ for breakfast.
○ bridge
○ dream
○ milk
● toast

1 Many people came to this country looking for greater _____.
○ snowstorm
○ farther
○ freedom
○ remember

2 A _____ track runs through the middle of town.
○ railroad
○ table
○ whisper
○ blame

3 My sister _____ interesting rocks.
○ stands
○ collects
○ grows
○ chews

4 Andy heard his father's _____ calling him from outside.
○ stand
○ voice
○ pipe
○ village

© Pearson Education 3

Baseline Group Test   **5**

A Students in Grade 3 are tested in phonics knowledge as well as vocabulary and comprehension.

B Vocabulary words are tested in context.

C Students read several passages and answer comprehension questions about them.

Samples are from Grade 3 test.

READING COMPREHENSION

Directions
Read each selection and answer the questions that follow. Fill in the circle beside the best answer to each question.

Ready for Blast-Off

Mom watched eagerly as the workers wheeled the new refrigerator into the kitchen. Katie and her brother Rory were excited too. The refrigerator came in a giant cardboard box. "What should we do with such a big box?" asked Katie.

Rory had an idea. "Let's make it into a spaceship!"

The children cut round windows and a door in the box. They drew buttons, levers, and knobs that would control the spaceship. When they were done, they crawled inside.

"Ready for blast-off!" shouted Rory, and Katie pushed a red button.

The children felt the box shudder, shake, and rise into the air. They peeked through the windows and saw dark sky and shiny stars. "We're really going to the moon!" Katie cried.

When the box landed with a bump, Rory and Katie crawled out. They explored the moon's craters and mountains. Everything was dark, dusty, and rocky.

"Let's stay here all night," suggested Rory.

"No, let's go home," replied Katie. "Mom will wonder where we are."

Rory followed her back to the box, still wishing they could stay longer. Katie pushed the red button again, and they were home just as Mom called them in for supper.

1 How did Katie and Rory feel about going to the moon?
○ bored
○ excited
○ relieved
○ disappointed

2 What part of this story could not really happen?
○ Two children decorate a big box.
○ A family gets a new refrigerator.
○ A mother calls her children for supper.
○ Two children go to the moon in a box.

3 Why did Katie want to go back home?
○ She didn't want her mother to worry.
○ She was hungry.
○ She was frightened.
○ She had homework to do.

4 Which of the following is the most likely reason the author wrote this story?
○ to describe the size of a refrigerator box
○ to give information about the moon
○ to explain how to make a rocket ship
○ to tell an entertaining story about two children

5 What did the children do after they explored the moon?
○ They watched workers deliver a refrigerator.
○ They drew buttons and levers on a box.
○ They went back home for supper.
○ They went to sleep in the box.

© Pearson Education

© Pearson Education 3

8   Baseline Group Test

Baseline Group Test   **9**

DIBELS (Dynamic Indicators of Basic Early Literacy Skills)

What is it?

- An optional assessment tool that is not a Scott Foresman product but is available through Scott Foresman

- A set of screening tasks that measure accuracy and fluency with connected text, vocabulary, and comprehension. Oral reading passages are given at each grade level to show which students are at risk for failure. A retelling of each passage targets those who do not comprehend.

Why would I choose it?

- To quickly group students who will need extra instruction—DIBELS provides benchmark goals that are highly predictive of reading success. It targets students who need strategic intervention and those who need intensive support in order to be successful.

- To establish which students need more diagnostic assessment to determine reading strengths and weaknesses

- To provide a record of students' continued growth throughout the year

- To provide information that will help you make instructional decisions for individual students and the classroom as a whole

What does the research say?

- Goals and cutpoints for third grade are well established by several years of study. Goals and cutpoints for Grades 4 through 6 are based on studies from Hasbrouck and Tindal (1992) and Fuchs, Fuchs, Hamlett, Walz, and Germann (1993). Goals and cutpoints may be further refined with ongoing research.

- DIBELS results correlate highly with outcome-based assessments. If students score at benchmark levels, they will probably also succeed on state-mandated tests.

- Technical reports, field studies, and a complete bibliography of over sixty studies on DIBELS are available on the DIBELS Web site: http://dibels.uoregon.edu

What does it test?

- In third grade, the DIBELS Oral Reading Fluency (DORF) and the accompanying Retell Fluency (RTF) measure fluency and accuracy with connected text, vocabulary, and comprehension. The Word Use Fluency (WUF) task measures vocabulary and oral language skills.

- In fourth and fifth grades, the DIBELS Oral Reading Fluency (DORF) and the accompanying Retell Fluency (RTF) measure fluency and accuracy with connected text, vocabulary, and comprehension.

How do I use it?

- Individually administer grade-appropriate benchmark tasks three times per year to monitor students and catch those at risk of failure. Each student reads three passages for one minute and retells each passage. The middle score is used to record the words per minute (WPM) a student reads correctly.

- Use alternate progress-monitoring forms (20 per grade level) more frequently to monitor the success of interventions with at-risk students.

- Allow 15 minutes per student to administer benchmark tasks three times per year.

- Use the DIBELS Web site to generate student and class reports.

When do I use it?

- Administer benchmark tasks to all students in the fall, winter, and spring, typically September, January, and May.

- Use progress-monitoring alternate forms of DIBELS tasks to assess at-risk students more frequently (monthly, bi-monthly, or weekly) to see whether specific instructional interventions are working.

How do I use the results?

- Look at entire class results to determine specific areas where most students are weak, and adjust teaching for those weak areas systematically and explicitly.

- Use results to plan additional assessment for at-risk students.

- Use results to aid in the formation of flexible groups.

- Use results to focus and plan instruction for flexible groups and for individuals.

- Use progress-monitoring results to adjust and refocus instruction on a regular basis.

- Use results to celebrate and inform students and parents about progress.

Weekly Selection Tests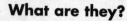

What are they?

- Tests designed to measure students' understanding of the content and vocabulary of the reading selections in *Scott Foresman Reading Street*
- Tests consisting of multiple-choice and constructed-response questions

Why would I choose them?

- To assess students' understanding of what they read on a frequent basis
- To assess students' understanding of the vocabulary words and target comprehension and strategies of the week
- To monitor students' progress during the week so that instruction can be modified if necessary

What do they test?

- Understanding of vocabulary words taught in a reading selection
- Comprehension of the reading selection through literal, inferential, and critical-analysis questions
- Use of reading skills and strategies taught in conjunction with the reading selection

When do I use them?

- Throughout the school year, typically mid-week after students have read a selection

How do I use them?

- The tests are designed to be group administered.

How do I use the results?

- To identify students who can successfully construct meaning from a reading selection and to identify which students need intervention
- To identify the specific comprehension skills a student has and has not mastered

Name _____ Volcanoes

VOCABULARY

Directions
Find the word or words with the same meaning as the underlined word. Mark the answer that means the same as the underlined word.

1 The cat hid beneath the sofa.
- ● under
- ○ next to
- ○ far from
- ○ behind

2 Each house had a brick chimney.
- ○ post used to build fences
- ○ box used for holding mail
- ● tower used to carry away smoke
- ○ wagon used for moving things

3 We study earthquakes.
- ○ the large loops that a planet makes as it goes around the sun
- ○ the turns that a planet makes that cause day and night
- ● the shifts in the crust of a planet that cause the ground to shake
- ○ the different layers of air that are found above a planet

4 Jean saw the fireworks.
- ● colorful lights that blow up in the sky
- ○ games that are played on a field
- ○ stars that can be seen from far away
- ○ drops of water that fall from clouds

5 The force knocked him down.
- ○ wind
- ○ crowd
- ● power
- ○ wave

© Pearson Education 3

Selection Test Unit 3 Week 5

Ⓐ

Name _____ Volcanoes

11 If there was less pressure on the inner core, it would probably
- ○ crack.   **[Draw Conclusions/Inferential]**
- ● melt.
- ○ explode.
- ○ split.

12 The author probably compared the plates to a jigsaw puzzle to help the reader
- ○ realize how dangerous the plates are.   **[Author's Purpose/Critical Analysis]**
- ○ know where the plates are located.
- ● understand what the plates look like.
- ○ figure out how thick the plates are.

13 According to the selection, where did most earthquakes occur? **[Generalize/Inferential]**
- ● where two plates met
- ○ under the mantle
- ○ in the ocean floor
- ○ near the inner core

14 Why do you think the author wrote this story? **[Author's Purpose/Critical Analysis]**
- ○ to show people why they should study volcanoes
- ○ to tell an exciting story about taking a trip into a volcano
- ● to give information about how volcanoes work
- ○ to describe what people should do if a volcano erupts

15 Which statement is an opinion? **[Fact and Opinion/Critical Analysis]**
- ○ The plates are located on the mantle.
- ○ Lava comes through cracks in the volcano.
- ○ The inner core is buried deep inside the planet.
- ● Volcanoes look beautiful from a distance.

© Pearson Education 3

Ⓑ

GO ON

Selection Test Unit 3 Week 5   **59**

Ⓐ Students are tested on all vocabulary words in a selection.

Ⓑ Comprehension items cover selection content as well as target skill.

Samples are from Grade 3 test.

© Pearson Education

Fresh Reads for Differentiated Test Practice

What are they?
- Tests that give students an opportunity to practice the comprehension skills of the week with a new selection, a "fresh read," matched to each student's instructional reading level
- Tests consisting of multiple-choice and constructed-response questions

Why would I choose them?
- To assess students's abilities to derive meaning from new selections that are at their instructional reading levels
- To retest a student's reading after administering the Weekly Selection Tests
- To check a student's reading rate

What do they test?
- The target and review comprehension skills and strategies for the week
- Comprehension of the reading selection through literal, inferential, and critical-analysis questions

When do I use them?
- Throughout the year, usually once a week after students have read a new selection aligned to their instructional level

How do I use them?
- The written tests are designed to be group administered
- Teachers choose which of the three leveled reading passages for the week to give to each student (Strategic Intervention, On-Level, or Advanced)
- Fluency checks are administered individually

How do I use the results?
- To gather additional information about a student's ability to comprehend a passage written at his/her instructional reading level
- To gather additional information about the specific comprehension skills a student has and has not mastered
- To monitor a student's progress in fluent reading

Name _____

Because of Winn-Dixie

Read the selection. Then answer the questions that follow.

Beach Party

Deb shook the crumbs off her beach towel and started off across the sandy beach to the lake. A strong wind was blowing, and the sun had disappeared behind black clouds. Very exciting weather, Deb thought.

"Where do you think you're going?" asked her mother, who was busy filling a beach bag. "That storm is coming in fast."

"Oh, Mom," said Deb. "Let's just stay till it starts to rain."

"No way," said her mother. "This is a dangerous place to be in a storm. Don't you know that lightning is attracted to water?"

Reluctantly Deb turned back. Quickly they finished packing and then carried everything to the car. Suddenly a flash of lightning lit up the sky, followed immediately by a crash of thunder. Rain began to fall in big fat drops that came faster and faster.

"Just in time," said Deb.

Turn the page.

Fresh Reads   Unit 1 Week 1 SI   1

Name _____

Because of Winn-Dixie

Read the selection. Then answer the questions that follow.

Missing Dog

Barry raced into the house, forgetting to close the back door. He was late for his baseball game and not thinking about his mother's warning about keeping that door closed so that Happy couldn't push it open and escape.

Barry changed into his uniform and grabbed his mitt. He was about to leave the house when he realized that he hadn't seen Happy. At the same instant, Barry noticed that the door was not quite closed. He called for the dog, but Happy did not appear. He checked the entire house, but the mutt had vanished. If anything happened to that dog, Barry thought, he would not forgive himself, and nobody else in the family would either.

Barry spent the next hour searching the neighborhood for Happy. He asked all his neighbors the same question: "Have you seen a little black-and-white mutt with big paws and enormous ears that is really friendly?"

They all shook their heads sympathetically.

Barry had just started designing a LOST DOG poster when his mother's car pulled into the driveway. He jogged over to her and was about to announce the bad news, when he caught sight of Happy sitting in the backseat. His mother rolled down the window and said, "Aren't you supposed to be at the baseball game?"

Turn the page.

Fresh Reads   Unit 1 Week 1 A   5

A

Name _____

Because of Winn-Dixie

Read the selection. Then answer the questions that follow.

Flapjacks

You may know them as flapjacks. But they go by other names as well, including	15
griddle cakes and hot cakes. The name depends on where you live. Still, most	29
Americans know a pancake when they see one.	37
This all-American food is delicious and easy to make. You can whip up a batter	52
in a matter of minutes. All you need is milk, an egg, butter, flour, baking powder,	68
and oil.	70
First, mix a tablespoon of baking powder with a half cup of flour. Next heat	85
together the egg with a half cup of milk and a quarter cup of oil. Slowly mix the dry	104
ingredients with the wet ones.	109
Now your batter is ready. Heat up a large frying pan and add two tablespoons	124
of butter. Pour spoonfuls of batter into the melted butter. Let the pancakes fry until	139
they are golden brown on the bottom. Flip them over and brown them on the other	155
side. Serve the pancakes hot with maple syrup, honey, or jam.	166
This simple recipe has many variations. Some people use buttermilk instead of	178
milk. Others use yogurt mixed with milk. Some cooks mix whole wheat, cornmeal,	191
or oats into the flour. Of course, choices for pancake toppings are endless. Fruit,	205
chocolate, and whipped cream are just a few favorites.	214
How do you like your hot cakes?	221

C

Turn the page.

Fresh Reads   Unit 1 Week 1 OL   3

Answer the questions below.

1 What do you do after you mix the egg, milk, and oil?
A   pour batter into the frying pan
B   mix dry and wet ingredients
C   add butter to the frying pan
D   add buttermilk to the mix

2 For cornmeal pancakes, when should you add the cornmeal?
F   after you heat the frying pan
G   after you add the toppings
H   when you mix the wet ingredients
J   when you mix the dry ingredients

3 What happens right after you add butter to the frying pan?
A   You add the flour.
B   You serve the pancakes.
C   The butter melts.
D   Pancake toppings are endless.

4 The author probably wrote this selection to
F   explain how to make pancakes.
G   convince the reader that pancakes are great for breakfast.
H   entertain the reader with an interesting story about pancakes.
J   express strong feelings about pancakes.

5 List the three main things you have to do to make pancakes. Use sequence words in your answer.
_____
_____
_____
_____
_____
_____

B

4   Fresh Reads   Unit 1 Week 1 OL

A Passages of different ability levels

B Questions on the target skill and review skill of the week

C Opportunity for fluency check

Samples are from Grade 4 Unit 1 test.

Formal Assessment   41

Unit Benchmark Tests

What are they?

- Tests designed to measure the student's ability to apply the target comprehension skills and other skills taught during the unit to a new reading selection

Why would I choose them?

- To assess students' understanding and use of specific skills
- To identify skill areas in which students need intervention and continued practice
- To know that there are sufficient items per individual skill to track a student's proficiency with that skill

What do they test?

In Grades 3–6

- Unit comprehension skills through literal, inferential, and critical-analysis questions
- Vocabulary strategies and skills
- Phonics in Grade 3 only
- Grammar, usage, and mechanics skills
- Ability to respond to a writing prompt
- Reading fluency (optional)

When do I use them?

- Throughout the year, at the end of each unit (about every six weeks)

How do I use them?

- The tests are designed to be group administered
- The optional reading fluency checks are individually administered

How do I use the results?

- To identify students who can successfully construct meaning from a reading selection and to identify students who need intervention
- To identify the specific skills students have and have not mastered

PART 1: COMPREHENSION

*D*irections
Many of the books we read as very young children teach us skills while entertaining us. Read about several of these popular books. Then do Numbers 1 through 11.

Reading to Learn

Did you read Eric Carle's *The Very Hungry Caterpillar* as a young child? If so, you're one of millions of children who enjoyed seeing the caterpillar munch through the book's pages.

And while you were munching through the book yourself, you were also learning. You were learning how to count as the caterpillar ate through one apple, then two pears, and so on. Even more, you were learning the days of the week, because the caterpillar ate something different each day. As the book concluded, you learned that a caterpillar spins a cocoon for itself and is next seen as a butterfly—and that is an important science lesson.

2   Benchmark Test Unit 3

Samples are from Grade 5 Unit 3 test.

B

3   Both *The Ugly Duckling* and *The Very Hungry Caterpillar* teach about
  A   time.
  B   science.
  C   history.
  D   mathematics.

4   Why did the author most likely include three lines from *Chicken Soup with Rice*?
  F   to demonstrate how easy it is to learn the months
  G   to give an example of poetry that teaches and is amusing
  H   to impress readers by quoting a well-known children's author
  J   to persuade readers with lines from a well-known book

5   Which of the following sentences is a statement of opinion?
  A   The rhymes make the months easy to remember.
  B   In *The Doorbell Rang*, the author shows the way division works.
  C   Millions of children have read *The Very Hungry Caterpillar*.
  D   There are many books written to help young children learn new skills.

6   Which of the following best describes this selection?
  F   historical nonfiction
  G   informational article
  H   realistic fiction
  J   folk tale

7   What is the main idea of this selection?
  A   A book can teach more than one thing.
  B   Science can be taught through books.
  C   One purpose of books is to entertain.
  D   Children learn things when they read.

8   Which of these conclusions can be drawn from the selection?
  F   Most important science lessons are taught in children's books.
  G   Most children's books are written in an entertaining way.
  H   Few children's books teach about how we view ourselves.
  J   Children's books can teach more than one thing.

4

C

PART 3: GRAMMAR, USAGE, MECHANICS

*D*irections
Mark your answer choice for Numbers 33 through 40.

Questions 33–35. Mark the answer that best completes the sentence.

33   The raindrops _____ cold.
  A   fell
  B   froze
  C   felt
  D   flied

34   Next week I _____ harder.
  F   had practiced
  G   will practice
  H   have practiced
  J   did practice

35   The teacher already _____ the lesson.
  A   had began
  B   beginned
  C   begun
  D   has begun

36   Which sentence is written correctly?
  F   Louis was sitting by the window watching the s
  G   The students set quietly, waiting for the teacher
  H   Sit the fence posts in a straight line.
  J   He told his dog to set.

D

PART 4: WRITING

PROMPT

Books can make us think, help us do things, and answer our questions. Artwork helps us use our senses.

The works of authors and artists help make our lives more enjoyable by giving us information, entertainment, or fresh ways of looking at things.

Choose two works produced by either an author or an artist, or one of each, and compare the ways their work has affected you.

CHECKLIST FOR WRITERS

_____ Did I think about two works by authors, artists, or both?

_____ Did I take notes for my paper about the same and different ways they have affected me?

_____ Did I write my comparison in a way that shows the similarities and differences?

_____ Did I use words and details that clearly express my ideas?

_____ Do my sentences make sense?

_____ Did I check my sentences for grammar and punctuation?

_____ Did I check my spelling?

_____ Did I make sure my paper is the way I want readers to read it?

Benchmark Test Unit 3   17

A   Students read selections in a variety of genres.

B   Students respond to multiple-choice and writing questions.

C   Vocabulary, Phonics (Grade 3), and Grammar, Usage, and Mechanics skills are tested.

D   Students produce original compositions relating selections in test to unit themes and writing instruction.

End-of-Year Benchmark Test

What is it?	• A test designed to measure students' understanding of skills, strategies, and critical-thinking skills taught throughout the year
	• A test consisting of multiple-choice and constructed-response questions
Why would I choose it?	• To assess students' understanding and use of specific skills
	• To identify skill areas in which students need intervention and continued practice
	• To measure students' understanding through an approach that integrates reading, writing, and themes in literature
What does it test?	**At Grades 3–6**
	• Comprehension skills through literal, inferential, and critical-analysis questions
	• Vocabulary strategies and skills
	• Phonics in Grade 3 only
	• Grammar, usage, and mechanics skills
	• Ability to respond to a writing prompt
	• Ability to make cross-text connections
	• Application of learning to a new situation
When do I use it?	• When students have completed all units in their textbook, usually at the end of the school year
How do I use it?	• The test is designed to be group administered
How do I use the results?	• To diagnose and record individual students' needs for the following school year
	• To inform and improve the delivery of curriculum and instruction
	• To determine students' overall grades
	• To provide helpful feedback to students and parents
	• To guide parents in working with their children during vacation, so learning continues throughout the summer months

A

PART 1: COMPREHENSION

Directions
Kayla wants to make the world a better place. Read the selection to see how she might solve her problem. Then answer Numbers 1 through 11.

Kayla's Problem

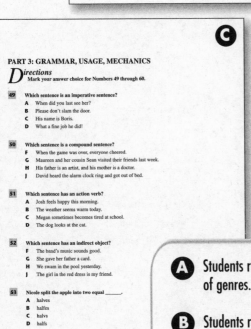

"It's just so frustrating to be in that fourteen-and-under category," muttered Kayla. "You want to do your bit to make the world a better place, but nobody lets you if you're not already fourteen."

"Well," said Kayla's mother, giving her daughter a meaningful glance, "you could always try cleaning up your room."

"Right, Mom, that's just what I had in mind as my contribution to the good of humanity."

"On a serious note, Kayla, I really appreciate all you do around here—taking care of your brothers after school and getting dinner ready for all of us."

"But I want to do something that helps other people, people outside our family. Whenever I try to volunteer, they tell me to call back when I'm finally fourteen—a whole year-and-a-half from now. And you remember the disaster of my attempts to convert Charlie into a therapy dog."

2   Benchmark Test   End-of-Year

B

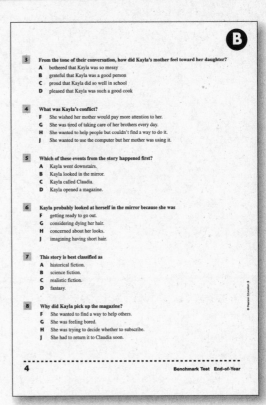

3 **From the tone of their conversation, how did Kayla's mother feel toward her daughter?**
A   bothered that Kayla was so messy
B   grateful that Kayla was a good person
C   proud that Kayla did so well in school
D   pleased that Kayla was such a good cook

4 **What was Kayla's conflict?**
F   She wished her mother would pay more attention to her.
G   She was tired of taking care of her brothers every day.
H   She wanted to help people but couldn't find a way to do it.
J   She wanted to use the computer but her mother was using it.

5 **Which of these events from the story happened first?**
A   Kayla went downstairs.
B   Kayla looked in the mirror.
C   Kayla called Claudia.
D   Kayla opened a magazine.

6 **Kayla probably looked at herself in the mirror because she was**
F   getting ready to go out.
G   considering dying her hair.
H   concerned about her looks.
J   imagining having short hair.

7 **This story is best classified as**
A   historical fiction.
B   science fiction.
C   realistic fiction.
D   fantasy.

8 **Why did Kayla pick up the magazine?**
F   She wanted to find a way to help others.
G   She was feeling bored.
H   She was trying to decide whether to subscribe.
J   She had to return it to Claudia soon.

4   Benchmark Test   End-of-Year

Samples are from Grade 6 end-of-year test.

C

PART 3: GRAMMAR, USAGE, MECHANICS

Directions
Mark your answer choice for Numbers 49 through 60.

49 **Which sentence is an imperative sentence?**
A   When did you last see her?
B   Please don't slam the door.
C   His name is Boris.
D   What a fine job he did!

50 **Which sentence is a compound sentence?**
F   When the game was over, everyone cheered.
G   Maureen and her cousin Sean visited their friends last week.
H   His father is an artist, and his mother is a doctor.
J   David heard the alarm clock ring and got out of bed.

51 **Which sentence has an action verb?**
A   Josh feels happy this morning.
B   The weather seems warm today.
C   Megan sometimes becomes tired at school.
D   The dog looks at the cat.

52 **Which sentence has an indirect object?**
F   The band's music sounds good.
G   She gave her father a card.
H   We swam in the pool yesterday.
J   The girl in the red dress is my friend.

53 **Nicole split the apple into two equal _____.**
A   halves
B   halfes
C   halvs
D   halfs

20

D

PART 4: WRITING

> **PROMPT**
>
> Alfred Nobel made a fortune from his invention of dynamite. The Song dynasty was marked by a series of important inventions. Your world is shaped by the many inventions around you. Think of an invention you consider important. Write an essay that will convince your reader of the importance of the invention you chose. Give reasons to support your viewpoint.

CHECKLIST FOR WRITERS

_____ Did I think about an invention that I consider important?

_____ Did I take notes for my paper about the reasons I think the invention is important?

_____ Did I organize my paper in a logical way?

_____ Did I use words and details that clearly express my ideas and that will convince others that the invention I chose is important?

_____ Do my sentences make sense?

_____ Did I check my sentences for grammar and punctuation?

_____ Did I check my spelling?

_____ Did I make sure my paper is the way I want readers to read it?

Benchmark Test   End-of-Year   23

A Students read selections in a variety of genres.

B Students respond to multiple-choice and writing questions.

C Vocabulary, Phonics (Grade 3), and Grammar, Usage, and Mechanics skills are tested.

D Students produce original compositions relating selections in test to unit themes and writing instruction.

Chapter 3

Classroom-based Informal Assessment Strategies and Tools

Overview

What is classroom-based assessment?

- A way to determine students' progress based on a regular process of observing, monitoring, and judging the quality of their work

- A system for examining students' work that focuses on formative and summative measures other than formal tests

- A strong basis for instructional decision making

- A means of helping students learn how to make judgments about the quality of their own work

What are the purposes of classroom-based assessments?

- To identify mastery

- To engage students and help develop positive attitudes

- To stress application and other reasoning skills

- To communicate progress to parents

- To identify areas in need of improvement

- To encourage students' self-assessment and evaluation

- To adjust instructional approaches (McMillan, 2001)

Why is classroom-based assessment so important?

- A formal assessment administered at the end of an instructional unit works like a snapshot of a moving body—capturing a moment in time. Because students' performance levels change rapidly at times, multiple assessments, similar to an album of snapshots or a video, are necessary.

> "…quality is the result of regular inspections (assessments) *along the way,* followed by needed adjustments based on the information gleaned from the inspections."
>
> (McTighe, 1997)

- High-quality work is most reliably achieved in small, consistent increases that occur over time. The goal is continuous improvement.

- Teachers can guide student learning better if they have up-to-date understanding of the student's current performance levels—wasting no time on skills students have already attained and focusing instead on the weaker areas.

- Frequent assessments give *all* students a more equitable opportunity to demonstrate their skills.

What techniques and tools are available?

Questioning Strategies (See pages 51–52)

- The ability to frame and ask powerful questions is an effective instructional and assessment strategy.

- Skillful questioning helps students recall what they know about a topic.

- Questions that require students to analyze information promote in-depth learning.

Tools for Getting to Know Your Students (See pages 53–60)

- Administering inventories, surveys, and checklists at the beginning of the school year helps you:
  - identify students' interests and attitudes about literacy
  - assess instructional and motivational needs of individual students
  - assess instructional needs of the class as a whole
  - learn specifics about students with particular needs, such as English language learners
  - make good instructional decisions

Ongoing Teacher Observation (See pages 61–68)

- Promotes continuous monitoring of student performance in the context of classroom activities

- Is grounded in the belief that students seldom attain their highest level of achievement in their first attempt

- Provides students with helpful feedback because it addresses learning while in progress, rather than after the fact

Student Self-Assessment (See pages 69–71)

- Use frequent monitoring to teach students how to assess their own work.

- Set goals with students and expect them to monitor their progress. This builds student independence in reading.

- Start as early as possible. Involve students productively in making judgments about quality as early as possible.

Student Portfolios (See pages 72–79)

- Portfolios provide a place to organize and keep the evidence of the student progress.

- Portfolios involve students in self-assessment; they evaluate portions of their own work and set goals for improvement.

- Portfolios usually contain student annotations, or "entry slips," identifying what each entry demonstrates—the basis for its inclusion in the portfolio.

> "Research on accomplished readers demonstrates that they are planful and aware and capable of online monitoring of their reading."
>
> (Afflerbach, 2001)

- Portfolios of student work are better when they result from a combination of "teacher direction and student selection." (Bailey and Guskey 2001)
- Portfolios may be organized in a number of different ways:
  - A gathering of products from a set of performance tasks
  - A collection of representative stages of work for certain products
  - A chronological representation of a learner's skill development in a subject or specific area of performance
  - Ascending order of quality to show growth over time (Danielson and Abrutyn 1997)
  - Descending order of quality to showcase highest quality work first time (Danielson and Abrutyn 1997)
  - A self-selected organization based on the student's intended use for the portfolio—perhaps to highlight specific skills

Teacher Summary Reports (See pages 80–83)

- Use observation sheets and other record forms to document and keep cumulative accounts of students as learners.

> "Any decision of consequence deserves more than one piece of evidence."
> (Pearson 1998)

What are some typical classroom-based assessment activities?

- Class discussions
- Speeches, oral readings, dramatizations, retellings
- Drawings, sculpture, and other artwork
- Graphic organizers
- Collaborative activities and projects
- Student response logs
- Student reflective essays

Where do I find classroom-based assessment activities in *Scott Foresman Reading Street?*

- The following teacher's edition features a variety of good opportunities to informally assess students:
  - Monitor Progress Boxes
  - Student Self-Monitoring
  - Guiding Comprehension Questions
  - Reading Fluency Assessment
  - Reader Response Questions
  - Practice for Standardized Tests
  - Retelling Scoring Rubrics
  - Writing Scoring Rubrics
  - Spelling Tests

When do I use these assessment activities?

- Use activities throughout the school year that measure students' growth and development to:
  - make instructional decisions about what to do next
  - help students check their progress
  - determine short-term instructional groupings (guided reading groups, for example)
  - help in differentiating instruction
  - check the effectiveness of instructional strategies

References

Afflerbach, P. *Reading Assessment and Accountability: Helping Children Learn to Self-assess Their Reading*. Presented at the CIERA Summer Institute, 2001.

Bailey, J. M., and T. R. Guskey. "Implementing Student-Led Conferences." In *Experts in Assessment Series*. Ed. T. R. Guskey, and R. J. Marzano. Thousand Oaks, CA: Corwin Press, Inc., 2001.

Danielson, C., and L. Abrutyn. *An Introduction to Using Portfolios in the Classroom*. Alexandria, VA: ASCD, 1997.

Gambrell, L. B., P. S. Koskinen, and B. A. Kapinus. "Retelling and the Reading Comprehension of Proficient and Less-Proficient Readers." *Journal of Educational Research*, vol. 84 (1991), pp. 356–363.

Gambrell, L. B., W. Pfeiffer, and R. Wilson. "The Effects of Retelling Upon Reading Comprehension and Recall of Text Information." *Journal of Educational Research*, vol. 78 (1985), pp. 216–220.

Keene, E. O., and S. Zimmermann. *Mosaic of Thought*. Portsmouth, NH: Heinemann, 1997.

McMillan, J. H. "Essential Assessment Concepts for Teachers and Administrators." In *Experts in Assessment Series*. Ed. T. R. Guskey, and R. J. Marzano. Thousand Oaks, CA: Corwin Press Inc., 2001.

McTighe, J. "What Happens Between Assessments?" *Educational Leadership*, vol. 54, no. 4 (1997); pp. 6–12.

Morrow, L. M. "Effects of Structural Guidance in Story Retelling on Children's Dictation of Original Stories." *Journal of Reading Behavior*, vol. 18, no. 2 (1986); pp. 135–152.

Moss, B. "Teaching Expository Text Structures Through Information Trade Book Retellings." *The Reading Teacher*, vol. 57, no. 8 (May 2004); pp. 710–718.

Pappas, C. C. "Fostering Full Access to Literacy by Including Information Books." *Language Arts*, vol. 68, no. 6 (October 1991); pp. 449–462.

Pearson, P. D. "Instruction and Assessment: Synergistic Energies or a Dysfunctional Family?" Presented at University of California, Berkeley, March 23, 1998.

Raphael, T. E. "Teaching Question Answer Relationships, Revisited." *The Reading Teacher*, vol. 39, no. 6 (February 1986); pp. 516–522.

Wixson, K. K., and M. N. Yochum. "Research on Literacy Policy and Professional Development: National, State, District, and Teacher Contexts." *Elementary School Journal*, vol. 105, no. 2 (November 2004); pp. 219–242.

Grades 3–6 Classroom-based Assessment: Techniques and Tools

Questioning Strategies

Why is questioning important?

- While asking questions is a routine practice for teachers, it is often overlooked as our most powerful tool for instruction and assessment.

- Artfully crafted questions engage students, focus their attention, stimulate their thinking, facilitate their understanding, and deepen their comprehension.

- Student self-generated questions improve learning and strengthen problem-solving and critical-thinking skills.

How do I use effective questioning strategies?

- Selectively choose questions for specific purposes (e.g., recall-level questions about sequence of ideas and analytic questions about the theme of a story).

- Ask questions that represent diverse thinking activities—recall, analysis, comparison, inference, and evaluation.

- Design questions that emphasize both content and the thinking needed to process the content, using such verbs as *list, define, compare, conclude,* and *defend.*

> "Our questions help us formulate our beliefs about teaching and learning, and those beliefs underlie our instructional decisions."
>
> (Keene & Zimmermann, 1997)

- Remember that when students are asked to analyze information, they will learn more than if asked simply to recall or identify information.

- Listen carefully to students' answers in order to shape skillful follow-up questions.

- Ask probing follow-up questions that help students extend their thinking and clarify and support their points of view.

- Allow wait time because it gives students time to think and provides answering opportunities for those who process more slowly.

- Model question-asking and question-answering behavior, and provide repeated opportunities for students to practice generating their own questions.

- Model questioning with a variety of texts, and, through reading conferences with the students, monitor their developing use of questioning.

- Guide students in understanding that through their own questions, they can actively regulate their reading and learning.

How does *Scott Foresman Reading Street* support effective questioning practices?

- Questioning strategies are based on a question-answer framework suggesting an interaction among the question, the text to which it refers, and the prior knowledge of the reader. (Raphael, 1986)

- Students are taught that answering comprehension questions in class and on tests demands thinking; they have to analyze the questions in order to provide the right answers.

- Students learn that answers to questions can be found **In the Book** and **In My Head.**

- **In the Book** questions can be:

  - **Right There** questions, which are *literal* and focus on ideas explicitly stated in the text. The words in the question may match the words in the passage.

  - **Think and Search** questions, which are also *literal* and require students to locate and integrate information from within different sections of the text.

- **In My Head** questions can be:

  - **Author and Me** questions, which are *inferential* in nature, requiring students to interpret information and connect themes and major ideas with their own background knowledge. The most demanding Author and Me questions necessitate use of *critical analysis* as readers evaluate and justify the purpose, content, and quality of text.

  - **On My Own** questions are not based on the text and can be answered from the students' general background knowledge and experience. These questions are often posed by teachers in order to activate prior knowledge before reading and/or to extend the learning beyond the lesson.

- The *Scott Foresman Reading Street* formal assessments offer students a variety of engaging narrative and expository texts, and students respond to test items designed to assess how they use their comprehension skills in constructing meaning.

- Literal, inferential, and critical-analysis questions on the formal assessments are based on the question-answer framework used in instruction and are similar to question types on high-stakes assessments.

- Daily practice in answering, analyzing, and asking Right There, Think and Search, and Author and Me questions will improve student achievement on high-stakes standardized tests.

Getting to Know Your Students

What is the purpose?

- To help you get to know your students and find a starting point in order to make good instructional decisions

- To help you gather information about students' reading, writing, speaking, listening, and viewing knowledge skills at the beginning of the year

- To gather specific information about students with particular needs, such as English language learners

What are my choices?

- Learn about students' interests

  - Have students complete a survey about their interests.

  - Have parents or caregivers complete a survey about their child's interests.

- Learn about students' needs

  - Use an interest inventory to poll students' feelings about reading and their general motivation to learn.

  - Have students complete a survey about learning styles.

  - Use a checklist to determine the level of students' English proficiency.

- Record what you have learned

  - Record the information you've gathered on the Student Portfolio Sheet.

When do I gather the information?

- During the first few weeks of the school year

How do I use the information?

- Use any or all of the provided materials to help you do the following:

  - Assess instructional and motivational needs of individual students.

  - Customize your instruction to meet the interests and needs of all the students in your classroom.

  - Group students according to their different starting points.

Myself as a Reader and Writer

What is it?	• An informal questionnaire that gives students an opportunity to tell you about their reading and writing interests
	• A tool that helps students reflect on reading and writing habits
What does it show?	• Genres and topics that are of interest to students
How do I use it?	• Have students complete the form early in the school year.
	• As an extension, ask students to exchange forms and find classmates with similar interests.
	• Attach the completed form to the Student Portfolio Sheet as additional information about each student.
	• Consider using the inventory during parent conferences.

A Checklist format is easy for students to complete and for you to interpret.

B Form probes students' interests in specific topics as well as genres.

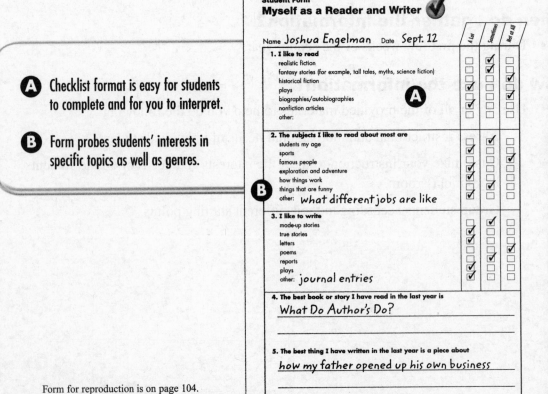

Form for reproduction is on page 104.
Spanish form for reproduction is on page 132.

Survey

How Do I Learn?

What is it?
- A form to help you recognize students with particular learning styles or preferences

What does it show?
- The survey can help you begin to identify
  - Students who learn best through sight or mental images (visual/spatial learners)
  - Students who learn best through body positions and movements (kinesthetic learners)
  - Students who learn best through interactions or negotiations with others (interpersonal learners)

How do I use it?
- Have students complete the form early in the school year
- Use the explanations below to help you begin to identify students with particular learning preferences

A An (a) response to questions 1 and 2 helps to identify students with strong visual/spatial or interpersonal preferences, respectively.

B Consistent responses to questions 3–5 point out
(a) visual/spatial learners;
(b) kinesthetic learners;
(c) interpersonal learners.

Student Form
How Do I Learn?

Name _Joshua Engelman_   Date _9/18_

1. Which statement is most true about you?
- a. ☐ I nearly always understand things better if I see a picture or diagram.
- b. ☐ When someone explains something, I usually understand it just by listening.
- c. ☑ Sometimes I need pictures to help me understand; other times I don't.

2. If you have a choice, you would rather work
- a. ☑ in a group with three or four others
- b. ☐ with one partner
- c. ☐ by yourself

3. You want to remember a story you read. The best way for you to do this would be to
- a. ☐ draw a picture of it
- b. ☑ act out a scene from it
- c. ☐ discuss it with a partner or group
- d. ☐ do this instead: _____

4. You go to a museum. The kind of exhibit you like best has
- a. ☐ a film to go with it
- b. ☑ levers and buttons you can play with
- c. ☐ a book where you can write what you liked and didn't like
- d. ☐ something else: _____

5. Your group is planning a presentation about castles for younger students. The part you would like to do best is
- a. ☐ design the invitations
- b. ☑ build a model of the castle
- c. ☐ talk to the students after the presentation to see how they liked it
- d. ☐ something else: _____

Form for reproduction is on page 109.
Spanish form for reproduction is on page 137.

3 • Informal Assessment

Reading and Me

What is it?
- An in-depth survey to gauge students' feelings about and confidence in their reading

What does it show?
- How students assess various aspects of their behavior as readers
- How students think they read various kinds of materials
- The value students place on reading

How do I use it?
- Administer the survey early in the school year.
- Evaluate students' responses in the four categories that are described on page 57.
- Attach the completed form to the Student Portfolio Sheet as additional information about each student.

Reading and Me ✓

Student Form
Reading and Me ✓

Name *Joshua Engelman*   Date *9/30*

Mark the box next to the answer that tells how you feel.

1. How often do you like to read?
- ☐ All of the time
- ☐ Sometimes
- ☑ Not too often
- ☐ Never

2. When I read I
- ☐ always try my best.
- ☑ try my best most of the time.
- ☐ don't try very hard.
- ☐ often give up.

3. In general, when I read I
- ☐ really enjoy it.
- ☐ think it's OK.
- ☑ don't like it very much.
- ☐ dislike it a lot.

4. I think reading is
- ☐ my favorite thing to do.
- ☐ one of my favorite things to do.
- ☑ not one of my favorite things to do.
- ☐ my least favorite thing to do.

5. I read
- ☐ a lot better than my classmates.
- ☐ a little better than my classmates.
- ☑ about the same as my classmates.
- ☐ worse than my classmates.

6. When I am reading by myself, I understand
- ☐ most of what I read.
- ☑ some of what I read.
- ☐ not much of what I read.
- ☐ very little of what I read.

7. I am
- ☐ a great reader.
- ☑ a good reader.
- ☑ an OK reader.
- ☐ a poor reader.

8. I care what other kids think about my reading.
- ☐ never
- ☐ not too often
- ☑ sometimes
- ☑ always

9. I think that reading is
- ☐ very easy.
- ☐ kind of easy.
- ☑ kind of hard.
- ☐ very hard.

10. When I read in school I usu
- ☐ feel good about it.
- ☑ feel OK about it.
- ☐ feel not too good about it.
- ☐ feel terrible about it.

Student Form
Reading and Me (continued) ✓

Mark the box next to the answer that tells how you feel.

11. I talk with my friends about the things that I read
- ☐ all of the time.
- ☐ sometimes.
- ☑ not too often.
- ☐ never.

12. People who read a lot are
- ☐ very interesting.
- ☑ kind of interesting.
- ☐ not very interesting.
- ☐ pretty boring.

13. I think that reading in school is
- ☐ very important.
- ☐ important.
- ☑ somewhat important.
- ☐ not too important.

14. I think that reading at home is
- ☐ very important.
- ☐ important.
- ☐ somewhat important.
- ☑ not too important.

15. I like getting a book for a present.
- ☐ all the time
- ☐ sometimes
- ☑ not very often
- ☐ never

16. I read newspapers
- ☐ very well.
- ☑ pretty well.
- ☐ not too well.
- ☐ not well at all.

17. I read schoolbooks
- ☐ very well.
- ☐ pretty well.
- ☑ not too well.
- ☐ not well at all.

18. I read comics
- ☑ very well.
- ☐ pretty well.
- ☐ not too well.
- ☐ not well at all.

19. I read magazines
- ☐ very well.
- ☑ pretty well.
- ☑ not too well.
- ☐ not well at all.

20. I read storybooks or novels
- ☐ very well.
- ☑ pretty well.
- ☐ not too well.
- ☐ not well at all.

A Items 1–4 probe students' motivation as readers.

B Items 6–10 get at students' feelings about their reading and how they measure themselves against other readers.

C Items 11–15 probe the value that students put on reading.

D Items 16–20 have students assess their ability at reading different kinds of materials.

3 • Informal Assessment

© Pearson Education

Forms for reproduction are on pages 105–106.
Spanish forms for reproduction are on pages 133–134.

Profile of English Language Learners

What is it?

- A form to help identify the strengths and needs of students whose first language is not English

What does it show?

- A second-language learner's proficiency with speaking, reading, and writing English

How do I use it?

- Identify students whose English proficiency you are uncertain about.

- Compile samples of the students as they speak, read aloud, and write.

- Use the form as a rough guideline to where students are and where they may need help.

- Use the criteria on the form to assess students' abilities in the various language areas.

What do I do next?

Consider one of these two options:

– Refer to the English Language Learners notes in the *Scott Foresman Reading Street* program teacher's edition, which offers modifications and extensions to help with many selections.

– Use the English Language Learners components of the program, which are aimed at developing skills for second-language learners as they read each program selection.

Teacher Form
Profile of English Language Learners ✔

Student: Jenny Chang

Trait	Mostly	Unevenly	Rarely	Date/Comment
Oral Language				
Uses names of many objects	✓			
Uses and understands basic everyday vocabulary	✓			
Speaks hesitantly, searching for words			✓	9/24 does this only when she is nervous
Speaks fluently but makes errors	✓			
Uses mostly present-tense verbs		✓		9/24 sometimes remembers tenses but often does not
Has trouble with irregular forms (standed, more slower)	✓			
Asks and answers simple questions	✓			
Follows simple directions		✓		10/1 sometimes has difficulty processing directions
Is able to explain events or ideas		✓		
Reading				
Recognizes basic sound/letter relationships in words	✓			
Follows text being read aloud	✓			
Needs pictures to comprehend text		✓		10/1 Jenny comprehends many basic texts.

A (near Trait column)
B (near Date/Comment column)

Teacher Form
Profile of English Language Learners (continued) ✔

Student:

Trait	Mostly	Unevenly	Rarely	Date/Comment	
Joins in choral reading	✓				
Retells predictable text	✓				
Recognizes many words by sight		✓		10/4–5	Jenny reads simple stories fairly well. Nonfiction is difficult. Sequence of all texts can be a problem.
Relies on print more than on illustrations		✓		10/4–5	
Retells beginning, middle, and end of things read		✓		10/4–5	
Writing					
Writes labels for pictures of people and actions	✓				
Uses single words or phrases to express ideas			✓		
Writes simple but understandable sentences		✓		10/8	
Spells simple words correctly		✓		10/8	
Makes up spellings showing correct sound/letter relationships		✓		10/8	Jenny will need consistent help with putting her ideas down on paper in a coherent, readable form.
Uses standard word order		✓		10/8	
Adds endings (-s, -es, 's, -ed, -ing) correctly		✓		10/8	
Understands basic capitalization and punctuation		✓		10/8	
Writes sentences demonstrating fluency and control of vocabulary		✓		10/8	

A Checklist format is easy to use.

B Space is provided for you to note your own responses.

© Pearson Education

Forms for reproduction are on pages 107–108.
Spanish forms for reproduction are on pages 135–136.

My Child as a Learner

What is it?	• A survey to help you get to know your students better from their families' perspective
	• An opportunity to establish a positive relationship with your students' families from the start
What does it show?	• Student behaviors that families observe at home
	• A family's view of a student as a learner
How do I use it?	• Send the survey home at the beginning of the school year with a cover letter explaining the value of family input.
	• Attach the completed form to the Student Portfolio Sheet as additional information about each student.
	• Use it during parent conferences.

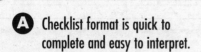 Checklist format is quick to complete and easy to interpret.

B Comments provide information specific to each student in your class.

C Additional comments let families offer information beyond the form.

Form for reproduction is on page 110.
Spanish form for reproduction is on page 138.

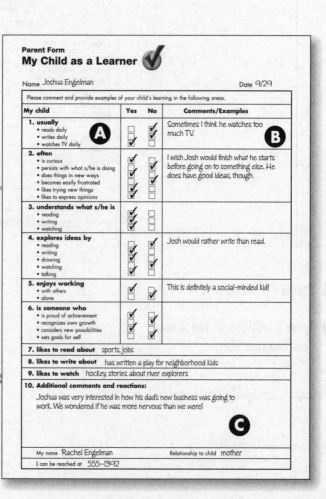

© Pearson Education

Ongoing Teacher Observation

What is it?

- Observation that occurs in the context of teaching or classroom activities
- A way to check students' progress on a daily or weekly basis
- The basis for developing a concrete plan for dealing with indivdual students' classroom strenghts or needs

How do I make observations?

- Choose one or more students to focus on each day.
- Select the literacy behavior, strategy, or skill that you wish to observe.
- Observe those students as they are participating in classroom activities.
- Using a clipboard, sticky note, customized form, or checklist, note a student's behavior or performance in the targeted skills.
- Include any comments, insights, or other information you regard as significant.
- Develop a record-keeping system that is convenient and informative for you.

Why should I record my observations?

- To remember information when you need to reflect on a student at the end of the day, week, grading period, or year
- As a helpful tool for presenting information to students, parents, and administrators
- For documentation when you need to explain why you've placed a student in a particular group or given a certain grade
- To plan strategies for intervening with students needing special attention

Running Record ✔

What is it?

- An individually administered procedure of recording and analyzing a student's specific reading behaviors

- A method of deciding whether a text is at the appropriate instructional level for a student

- A means of determining the level of support a student will need while reading the material

What does it show?

- Teachers who administer regular running records gather evidence about the following:

  - reading strategies a student uses and how he or she uses them to derive meaning

  - decoding and word recognition strategies

  - comprehension of text

  - fluency and oral reading skills

When do I use it?

- As often as necessary to get a clear and ongoing picture of a student's precise reading behaviors (for example, at the beginning or end of a unit or grading period when you need to report progress to interested parties)

How do I use it?

- Use an excerpt from *Scott Foresman Reading Street,* from a trade book, or any other text that is at an appropriate reading level for the student.

- Observe the student closely as he or she reads aloud, and code behaviors on your copy of the text.

- Make a photocopy for yourself of the passage you will have the student read.

- Indicate the number of the text line, and note the miscues, or errors, that are made, as well as the strategies the student is using.

- Use the following notations and symbols:

- Accurate Reading (✓) – Record a check for each word read accurately. The line of checks matches the layout of print.

- Substitutions – Write the substituted word above the text word. Cross out the text word. If it is a nonsense word, write it phonetically.

- Self-correction (*sc*) – Write *sc* in a circle next to the corrected word/text.

- Insertions (^) – Write the inserted word/phrase. Mark each insertion with a caret. Include any repetitions of words.

- Omissions – Write the word/phrase and circle the part(s) omitted.

- Hesitations – Write a capital *H* above and underline the word the student hesitates over. Wait a few seconds before providing the answer.

- Mispronunciation/misreading – Write the student's pronunciation above the word.

Name *Susan*   *9/4/2009*

Flapjacks

✓ ✓ ✓ ✓ ✓ ✓ ✓ ✓ ✓ ✓ ✓ ✓ ✓ ✓
You may know them as flapjacks. But they go by other names as well, including | 15

H ✓ ✓ ✓ ✓ ✓ ✓ ✓ ✓ ✓ ✓ ✓*too* ✓ ✓
griddle cakes and hot cakes. The name depends on where you live. Still, most | 29
                                                                    ^

✓ ✓ ✓ ✓ ✓ ✓ ✓ ✓
Americans know a pancake when they see one. | 37

✓ ✓ ✓ *delicate* ✓ ✓ ✓ ✓ ✓ ✓ ✓ ✓
This all-American food is delicious and easy to make. You can whip up a batter | 52

✓ ✓ ✓ ✓ ✓ ✓ ✓ ✓ ✓ ✓ ✓ ✓ ✓ ✓ ✓
in a matter of minutes. All you need is milk, an egg, butter, flour, baking powder, | 68

✓ ✓
and oil. | 70

✓ ✓ ✓ ✓ ✓ ✓ *and*✓ ✓ ✓ ✓ ✓ ✓
First, mix a tablespoon of baking powder ~~with~~ a half cup of flour. Next beat | 85

✓ ✓ ✓ ✓ ✓ ✓ ✓ ✓ ✓ ✓ ✓ ✓ ✓ ✓ ✓ ✓
together the egg with a half cup of milk and a quarter cup of oil. Slowly mix the dry | 104

(sc) ✓ ✓ ✓ ✓
ingredients with the wet ones. | 109

$$\frac{109 - 5}{109} = 95\%$$

$$\frac{\text{Total number of words read} - \text{number of errors}}{\text{Total number of words read}} = \text{percentage score}$$

Teacher Form
Retelling

What is retelling?	• A post-reading recall of what students can remember from reading or listening to a particular text • An oral or written recounting of narrative or expository text in a student's own words
What does it show?	• Students' ability to understand narrative text elements and author's purpose, and to connect stories to personal experiences and other texts • Students' ability to understand expository text—the relationship of main ideas and details, organizational structure, author's purpose, and inferences—and to connect texts to personal experiences and prior knowledge (Moss, 2004)
What does the research say?	• Several researchers have found that using retellings improves student understanding of text. (Gambrell, Koskinen & Kapinus, 1991; Gambrell, Pfeiffer & Wilson, 1985; Morrow, 1986)

How do I do it?	• In preparation:
	
	  – Have students attempt retelling narrative or expository text only after you have taught and modeled the procedure and they understand the task.
	
	  – Have students practice in groups before retelling for assessment purposes.
	
	  – Teach text structures (narrative and expository) separately to avoid confusing students.
	
	• For oral retellings, read the passage aloud to the student, or have the student read the selected text. Remind the student to remember everything he/she has heard or read. Then, ask the student to tell you everything about what he/she read.
	
	• At the end of the retelling, use follow-up questions (e.g., main idea, author's purpose, personal response) to gain deeper understanding of the student's comprehension.

- For written retellings, read the text aloud to students, or ask them to read it silently. Remind the students to remember everything they can. Immediately after reading, have students write out what they remember about the text.

How do I use the Retelling Forms?

- Record your scores and observations on either the narrative or the expository checklist. Try to record at least one narrative and one expository retelling from each student per unit.

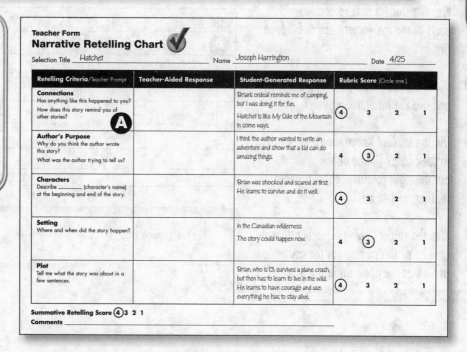

Teacher Form
Expository Retelling Chart ✓

Selection Title _Find the Constellations_   Name _Robert Williams_   Date _2/17_

Retelling Criteria/Teacher Prompt	Teacher-Aided Response	Student-Generated Response	Rubric Score (Circle one.)			
Connections Did this selection make you think about something else you have read? What did you learn about as you read this selection?		I thought of our science chapter on the solar system. I learned where the constellations are.	④	3	2	1
Author's Purpose Why do you think the author wrote this selection?		He told about how he likes looking at stars.	4	3	②	1
Topic What was the selection mostly about?		Constellations — What they look like and where and when to see them.	④	3	2	1
Important Ideas What is important for me to know about _____ (topic)?		The stars are in different places at different times of the year.	④	3	2	1
Conclusions What did you learn from reading this selection?		How to find different constellations.	④	3	2	1

Summative Retelling Score ④ 3 2 1
Comments _____

Ⓐ Criteria reflects comprehension skills.

Ⓑ Criteria helps students pinpoint key information

Teacher Form
Narrative Retelling Chart ✓

Selection Title _Hatchet_   Name _Joseph Harrington_   Date _4/25_

Retelling Criteria/Teacher Prompt	Teacher-Aided Response	Student-Generated Response	Rubric Score (Circle one.)			
Connections Has anything like this happened to you? How does this story remind you of other stories?		Brian's ordeal reminds me of camping, but I was doing it for fun. Hatchet is like My Side of the Mountain in some ways.	④	3	2	1
Author's Purpose Why do you think the author wrote this story? What was the author trying to tell us?		I think the author wanted to write an adventure and show that a kid can do amazing things.	4	③	2	1
Characters Describe _____ (character's name) at the beginning and end of the story.		Brian was shocked and scared at first. He learns to survive and do it well.	④	3	2	1
Setting Where and when did the story happen?		In the Canadian wilderness The story could happen now.	4	③	2	1
Plot Tell me what the story was about in a few sentences.		Brian, who is 13, survives a plane crash, but then has to learn to live in the wild. He learns to have courage and use everything he has to stay alive.	④	3	2	1

Summative Retelling Score ④ 3 2 1
Comments _____

Forms for reproduction are on pages 111–112.
Spanish forms for reproduction are on pages 139–140.

3 • Informal Assessment

Reading Strategy Assessment

What is it?

- A form to use at the end of each grading period to help you synthesize the information you've gathered about a student's reading progress

What does it show?

- A student's reading growth and progress over the course of a grading period
- A student's knowledge and use of reading strategies, including self-assessment

How do I use it?

- Use the checklist to summarize a student's progress or to help you transfer information to a more traditional reporting form.

A Criteria help you synthesize the information you've compiled from any of the forms and checklists you used throughout the grading period.

Form for reproduction is on page 125.
Spanish form for reproduction is on page 153.

Teacher Form

Reading Strategy Assessment ✓

Student _Kathy Noonan_   Date _11/3_
Teacher _Mrs. Hill_   Grade _4_

		Proficient	Developing	Emerging	Not showing yet
Building Background	Previews	✓			
Comments:	Ask questions	✓			
Is usually very interested	Predicts	✓			
in what she is reading.	Activates prior knowledge	✓			
A	Sets own purposes for reading	✓			
	Other:				
Comprehension	Retells/Summarizes	✓			
Comments:	Questions and evaluates ideas		✓		
Needs to work on	Paraphrases	✓			
decoding skills. Kathy	Rereads/reads ahead for meaning			✓	
comprehends well	Visualizes	✓			
unless vocabulary	Uses decoding strategies		✓		
is problematic. Is	Uses vocabulary strategies		✓		
sometimes reluctant to	Understands key ideas in a text		✓		
try new approaches	Other:				
(e.g. reading ahead).					
Fluency	Adjusts reading rate	✓			
Comments:	Reads for accuracy		✓		
Reads dialogue with	Uses expression	✓			
expression.	Other:				
Connections	Relates text to text	✓			
Comments:	Relates text to self	✓			
Interested in pursuing a	Relates text to world	✓			
variety of materials.	Other: explores genres	✓			
Self-Assessment	Is aware of: Strengths		✓		
Comments:	Needs		✓		
Thinks that she reads	Improvement/Achievement		✓		
more than she does.	Sets and implements learning goals	✓			
Kathy shys away from	Maintains logs, records, portfolio	✓			
collaborative learning	Works with others			✓	
activities.	Shares ideas and materials		✓		
	Other: accepts suggestions for improvement		✓		

Teacher Form
Writing Strategy Assessment

What is it?

- A form to use at the end of each grading period to help you synthesize the information you've gathered about a student's writing progress

What does it show?

- A student's writing growth and progress over the course of a grading period based on the 6-trait writing system
- A student's knowledge and use of writing strategies, including self-assessment

How do I use it?

- Use the checklist to summarize a student's progress or to help you transfer information to a more traditional reporting form.

A Criteria help you synthesize the information you've compiled from any of the forms and checklists you used throughout the grading period.

Teacher Form
Writing Strategy Assessment

Student: Kari Snow   Date: 10/15
Teacher: Ms. Brewer   Grade: 4

		Competent	Developing	Emerging	Not showing trait
Ideas Comments: needs to expand details	Identifies purpose in opening paragraph	☑	☐	☐	☐
	States main idea	☑	☐	☐	☐
	Details support main idea	☐	☑	☐	☐
	Gathers ideas and information	☐	☑	☐	☐
	Conclusion reinforces main idea	☐	☑	☐	☐
	Other:				
Organization Comments: difficulty with conclusions	Product of writing process	☑	☐	☐	☐
	Has a clear beginning, middle, and end	☐	☑	☐	☐
	Begins with a topic sentence	☐	☑	☐	☐
	Uses transitions between sentences and paragraphs	☐	☑	☐	☐
	Uses order words (first, then, after, finally)	☐	☑	☐	☐
	Other:				
Voice Comments: doesn't have a grasp on voice	Speaks directly to audience	☐	☑	☐	☐
	Voice matches writer's purpose	☐	☑	☐	☐
	Shows rather than tells	☐	☑	☐	☐
	Writer's feelings and personality emerge	☐	☑	☐	☐
	Keeps reader's attention	☐	☑	☐	☐
	Other:				
Word Choice Comments:	Uses vivid words to elaborate ideas	☑	☑	☐	☐
	Avoids slang and jargon	☐	☑	☐	☐
	Uses strong images or figurative language	☐	☑	☐	☐
	Uses action verbs versus linking verbs	☐	☑	☐	☐
	Uses new words to express ideas	☐	☑	☐	☐
	Other:				
Sentence Fluency Comments:	Expresses thoughts in lively, varied sentences	☐	☑	☐	☐
	Mixes short and long sentences	☑	☐	☐	☐
	Includes questions, commands, and exclamations	☑	☐	☐	☐
	Sentences flow logically from one to another	☐	☑	☐	☐
	Avoids choppy and wordy sentences	☐	☑	☐	☐
	Other:				
Conventions Comments: great spelling and grammar	Subjects and verbs are in agreement	☑	☐	☐	☐
	Uses correct punctuation for grade level	☑	☐	☐	☐
	Capitalizes proper nouns and sentence beginnings	☑	☐	☐	☐
	Forms plurals of nouns	☑	☐	☐	☐
	Words are spelled correctly	☑	☐	☐	☐
	Other:				

Form for reproduction is on page 126.
Spanish form for reproduction is on page 154.

Teacher Form
Cumulative Folder Form

What is it?
- A cumulative record of a student's reading progress, to be placed in the student's permanent record that follows a student from year to year

What does it show?
- The most basic and permanent information on how the student performed during a school year, namely, scores for the Baseline Test, Unit Benchmark Tests, and End-of-Year Benchmark Test, the group in which the student received instruction, and any additional comments a teacher wants to make

How do I use it?
- Record scores and comments from unit to unit.
- Place the form into the student's cumulative folder at the end of the school year.

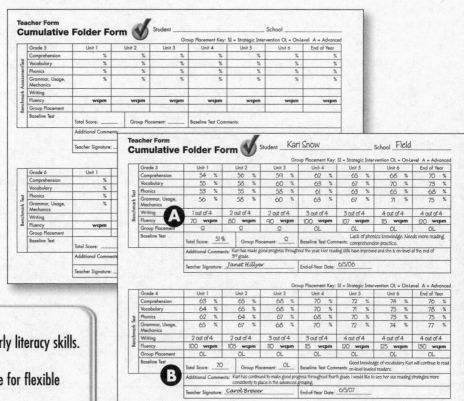

A Categories reflect early literacy skills.

B Scores serve as guide for flexible group placement.

Forms for reproduction are on pages 127–128.

Chapter 4

Assessment of English Language Learners

Overview

What are the unique challenges in assessing English language learners?

- Many English language learners may quickly master *social* English, the conversational language skills and conventions used in everyday interactions with classmates.

- These same learners frequently encounter difficulty with the *academic* English found on formal assessments.

- The structure of academic English is complex, for example, fiction and nonfiction text structures, paragraph organization, and syntax, including prepositional phrases, introductory clauses, and pronoun references.

- The vocabulary of academic English consists of specialized meanings of common words, abstract concepts and multiple-meaning words, and words based on Latin and Greek roots. (Bielenberg, 2001)

- The topics and concepts of comprehension passages are frequently unfamiliar, and the purposes of assessment tasks divorced from real-life contexts can be difficult to perceive.

- Formal assessments often fail to reflect the diverse cultural and linguistic experiences of English language learners, and then have limited value for helping teachers select appropriate instructional strategies. (Garcia, 1994)

How are *Scott Foresman Reading Street* assessments sensitive to the needs of English language learners?

- Both formal and informal classroom-based *Scott Foresman Reading Street* assessments help teachers monitor growth in the basic reading and expression skills of alphabetic understanding, decoding, sight vocabulary, and grammar, along with measurement of the more complex skills of fluency, comprehension, and vocabulary.

- Reading comprehension test passages reflect diverse ethnic and cultural experiences.

- Texts are matched to the age, interest, and background knowledge of the students.

- Most assessment tasks are embedded in contexts with which students have familiarity. The comprehension assessments are generally based on themes and topics explored in instruction; vocabulary is assessed within the context of the passage; and writing tasks relate to main ideas of the texts.

- Visual cues, pictures, and other non-print features accompany assessment passages.

- The language of the test directions and assessment items is straightforward and unambiguous.

What instructional strategies will help prepare my English language learners for formal assessments?

- Pre-teach the "language of tests" encountered in directions and test items, including:

  - Question words: *who, what, which, where, when, why,* and *how*

  - Emphasis words: *not, except, most likely, probably, major, both, neither, either, most,* and *least*

  - Action words: *explain, describe, discuss, persuade,* and *support with experience*

- Teach use of context clues to interpret meaning of unfamiliar terms.

- Highlight and discuss routinely the *academic* language, vocabulary, syntax, and narrative and expository text structures encountered in textbooks and trade books.

- Coach students in oral and written retelling, so they develop a "sense" of text types, features, conventions, and organization. English language learners, relate to the concrete nature of informational text, and expository retellings familiarize them with the common text structures, such as sequence, description, classification, compare/contrast, cause/effect, and problem/solution. In addition, retelling is an important first step to summarization, a critical skill for success in literacy.

- Provide regular opportunities for meaningful oral language experiences in which English language learners participate in discussion of important topics and perform the activities required on tests, such as explaining, describing, and stating and supporting opinions. Encourage them to use vocabulary that will support academic language development.

- Download and examine released forms of state and standardized assessments, reviewing the various item constructions and test vocabulary. Model and discuss the thinking steps involved in responding to both multiple-choice and constructed-response items.

- Read aloud, think aloud, and model the purposeful and strategic behaviors of effective readers.

- Provide repeated opportunities for practicing all the techniques above.

What accommodations are appropriate to use with the *Scott Foresman Reading Street* formal assessments?

- Accommodating the needs of English language learners ensures fairness and full participation in the formal assessments. A general rule of thumb is to use the same accommodations in testing situations as used in instruction. For instance, if students receive part of their instruction in their native language, then it is appropriate to translate test directions and comprehension questions into the student's first language.

- Acceptable accommodations might include:

- providing additional testing time and allowing frequent or extended breaks

- administering the tests at times most beneficial to the students

- administering the tests in small groups or in one-on-one settings

- reading test directions to students in English (or in the students' native languages, if this is possible), and repeating as often as needed

- simplifying the language and sentence structure of test directions

- requesting that students restate and clarify test directions in their own words

- discussing the pictures and any graphics, such as maps, to ensure that students can interpret them

- allowing the use of bilingual word-for-word translation dictionaries

- reading comprehension questions orally to students in English or in their native languages

- allowing students to respond orally to questions or dictate answers for transcription

- In providing accommodations to students, it is important not to compromise the intent of the assessment. It is never appropriate to read the reading comprehension *passages* or the vocabulary and grammar questions to students in English or their native languages; nor is it allowable to transcribe students's oral responses to the writing prompts. These practices alter the constructs of the assessments. For example, the reading comprehension assessments are designed to measure both word recognition and understanding, so reading the selections to students actually changes the intent of the test.

What are the *best* ways to assess the strengths and needs of English language learners?

- Through informal and ongoing classroom-based assessment, teachers can observe, monitor, and judge the quality of students' work.

- Multiple assessments mirror the learning process, while single assessments capture one moment at a time, much like the difference between a video or album of photographs and a single snapshot.

- Observing small, consistent increases in learning over time is most reliable. The goal is continuous improvement.

- Frequent monitoring addresses learning in progress, allows for correction of misconceptions as they occur, and provides helpful feedback to English language learners.

- Teaching students to self-assess their reading progress helps to build independence in language and learning.

- Authentic assessment activities enhance, rather than diminish, instructional time, because they are part of instruction. Activities include classroom observation, language-experience stories, storytelling or writing, tape recordings of oral reading, reading-response logs, and journals. (Garcia, 1994)

References

Bielenberg, B., and L. W. Fillmore. "The English They Need for the Test." *Educational Leadership,* 62 (4) (2004), pp. 45–49.

Garcia, G. E. "Assessing the Literacy Development of Second-Language Students: A Focus on Authentic Assessment." *Kids Come in All Languages: Reading Instruction for ESL Students,* Spangenberg-Urbshat, K. and R. Pritchard, eds., pp. 180–205. International Reading Association, 1994.

Lenters, K. "No Half Measures: Reading Instruction for Young Second-Language Learners." *The Reading Teacher*, 58 (2004), pp. 328–336.

Moss, B. "Teaching Expository Text Structures Through Information Trade Book Retellings." *The Reading Teacher*, 57 (2004), pp. 710–718.

Zwiers, J. "The Third Language of Academic English." *Educational Leadership,* 62 (4) (2002), pp. 60–63.

Teacher Form
Observing English Language Learners

What is it?	• A form to record your ongoing observations about how English language learners process what they read
What does it show?	• How English language learners use strategies to make sense of materials they read • Students' growth and development in processing what they read
How do I use it?	• Work with students individually as they read a new selection. • Record your observations about how students deal with new words and concepts. • Continue to review and record students' behaviors periodically as needed. • Consider using the information on the form in parent conferences.

A Behaviors identify common strategies for success in reading a new language.

B Space is provided to record students' development over time.

Teacher Form
Observing English Language Learners ✔

Student: Jenny Chang

Behaviors Observed	Date: 10/17			Date: 11/3			Date:			Date:		
The student	Yes	No	Sometimes	Yes	No	Sometimes	Yes	No	Sometimes	Yes	No	Sometimes
• uses context clues to figure out new words		✔				✔						
• uses prior knowledge to figure out new words			✔			✔						
• uses visuals to decipher meaning	✔					✔						
• uses strategies to decipher meaning			✔	✔								
• can identify the strategies he or she is using			✔			✔						
• understands why he or she is using a particular strategy	✔			✔								
• assesses his or her own progress	✔			✔								
• generally understands what the class is reading			✔			✔						

General Comments

10/17: Jenny needs to get used to using strategies and to know how and why she is using them.

11/3: A lot of progress in self-monitoring and in understanding texts!

Form for reproduction is on page 115.
Spanish form for reproduction is on page 143.

4 • ELL Assessment

ELL Assessment 89

Profile of English Language Learners

What is it?

- A form to help identify the strengths and needs of students whose first language is not English

What does it show?

- A second-language learner's proficiency with speaking, reading, and writing English

How do I use it?

- Identify students whose English proficiency you are uncertain about.

- Compile samples of the students as they speak, read aloud, and write.

- Use the criteria on the form to assess students' abilities in the various language areas.

- Use the form as a rough guideline of where students are and where they may need help.

What do I do next?

Consider one of these two options:

- Refer to the English Language Learners notes in the *Scott Foresman Reading Street* program teacher's edition, which offers modifications and extensions to help with many selections.

- Use the English Language Learners components of the program, which are aimed at developing skills for second-language learners as they read each program selection.

Teacher Form
Profile of English Language Learners ✓

Student: Jenny Chang

Trait	Mostly	Unevenly	Rarely	Date/Comment
Oral Language				
Uses names of many objects	✓			
Uses and understands basic everyday vocabulary	✓			
Speaks hesitantly, searching for words			✓	9/24 does this only when she is nervous
Speaks fluently but makes errors	✓			
Uses mostly present-tense verbs		✓		9/24 sometimes remembers tenses but often does not
Has trouble with irregular forms (standed, more slower)	✓			
Asks and answers simple questions	✓			
Follows simple directions		✓		10/1 sometimes has difficulty processing directions
Is able to explain events or ideas		✓		
Reading				
Recognizes basic sound/letter relationships in words	✓			
Follows text being read aloud	✓			
Needs pictures to comprehend text		✓		10/1 Jenny comprehends many basic texts.

Teacher Form
Profile of English Language Learners (continued) ✓

Student:

Trait	Mostly	Unevenly	Rarely	Date/Comment
Joins in choral reading	✓			
Retells predictable text	✓			
Recognizes many words by sight		✓		10/4–5
Relies on print more than on illustrations		✓		10/4–5 Jenny reads simple stories fairly well. Nonfiction is difficult. Sequence of all texts can be a problem.
Retells beginning, middle, and end of things read		✓		10/4–5
Writing				
Writes labels for pictures of people and actions	✓			
Uses single words or phrases to express ideas			✓	
Writes simple but understandable sentences		✓		10/8
Spells simple words correctly		✓		10/8
Makes up spellings showing correct sound/letter relationships		✓		10/8 Jenny will need consistent help with putting her ideas down on paper in a coherent, readable form.
Uses standard word order		✓		10/8
Adds endings (-s, -es, 's, -ed, -ing) correctly		✓		10/8
Understands basic capitalization and punctuation		✓		10/8
Writes sentences demonstrating fluency and control of vocabulary		✓		10/8

A Checklist format is easy to use.

B Space is provided for you to note your own responses.

Forms for reproduction are on pages 107–108.
Spanish form for reproduction is on page 135–136.

4 • ELL Assessment

Chapter 5 Grading

Overview

What are the purposes of grading?

- The primary goals are to:
  - Support learning and to encourage students' success
  - Inform students, parents, teachers, and others about students' achievement of standards
- Many experts also suggest that a fair grading system can also serve as an effective technique for motivation. (Guskey, 2002)

How do the terms "evaluation," "score," and "grade" differ?

- **Evaluation** is the assignment of value to the evidence of learning provided by the student through formative or summative assessments.

- A **score** or **mark** is the evaluative number or label given on any single test or assignment.

- A **grade** is the number or letter reported at the end of an instructional period as a summary statement of a student's performance. A grade may be based on multiple scores.

What are some general guidelines for grading?

- Academic achievement is the major factor on which grades should be based. It is appropriate to provide feedback to students on their effort, behavior, ability, and attendance, but these factors should be documented and reported separately. (Marzano, 2000)

- Grades should communicate achievement of clear and public learning targets or standards. (O'Connor, 2002)

- Expectations for grading should be discussed with students at the beginning of instruction. Explain what you value and how you want learning demonstrated. Show models of students' work at different grade and score points. Hold to your process!

- Grades alone are not always helpful, but grades accompanied by honest and descriptive feedback can provide incentives for increasing learning effort. (Afflerbach, 1993)

What are some opportunities for grading in *Scott Foresman Reading Street?*

- The program offers you opportunities to grade student work on a variety of activities, including:
  - Daily classwork
  - Individual or group activities and projects
  - Writing assignments
  - Pages from the Practice Book
  - Pages from Fresh Reads for Differentiated Test Practice
  - Speeches and other oral presentations
  - Graphic or artistic representations
  - Weekly Selection Tests
  - Unit Benchmark Tests
  - End-of-Year Tests

What tools are available to make grading easier?

- The following features can all facilitate grading:
  - The teacher's edition includes rubrics to help you determine grades for students' compositions.
  - Unit Benchmark Tests are accompanied by suggestions on how to convert raw scores into grades.
  - The Creating a Rubric form lets you create your own criteria and grading scales for other kinds of assignments.

Why are rubrics effective grading guides?

- Rubrics allow you to grade fairly, because the evidence for grading (strengths and weaknesses) is clearly specified for students and parents.

- Rubric criteria must be aligned with learning targets and standards.

- Rubrics are "coaching tools" that guide students in revising their work and improving learning.

Must all work be graded?

- It is not mandatory, nor beneficial for students, to grade every piece of work. Summative assessments should be graded because they measure achievement of learning targets. When you grade formative assessments designed to monitor learning, you're actually grading how fast students achieve the standards. For example, you may want to assign certain Practice Book pages simply to help students better understand concepts, not to assign grades.

Is any grading system or scale recommended?

- Dividing a student's score on an assignment or test by the total possible score is one common way of determining a grade. What percentage score equals an A, B, or C, however, may vary widely from school to school. You should follow your school's or district's recommendations.

How important is it to have a schoolwide or district-wide grading policy in place?

- It is very important to have an agreed-upon system to ensure that grading practices are consistently applied within the building and the district. If your school district does not have a general policy for converting scores to grades, or if the existing one is ambiguous or timeworn, you might propose that a group be convened for a period of time to study common issues related to grading and reporting. The resources listed in the bibliography for this chapter provide a good starting point.

References

Afflerbach, P. "Report Cards and Reading." *The Reading Teacher,* 46 (1993), pp. 457–465.

Guskey, T. R. *How's My Kid Doing? A Parent's Guide to Grades, Marks, and Report Cards.* Jossey-Bass, 2002.

Marzano, R. J. *Transforming Classroom Grading.* Association for Supervision and Curriculum Development, 2000.

O'Connor, K. *How to Grade for Learning.* Skylight Professional Development, 2002.

Creating a Rubric

What is it?

- A form that may be used for evaluation of reading, writing, speaking, listening, or viewing assignments
- A tool that allows you to focus assessment on the key concepts you emphasized during instruction

What does it show?

- How well a student exhibits his or her understanding of the key features of the assignment
- Areas in which the student may require additional instruction

How do I use it?

- Decide which assessment criteria are most relevant to a particular assignment. List them in the Features column.
- Rate and comment on those features as you assess the assignment.
- See the three forms that follow for converting these ratings to grades.

A The open-endedness of this form allows you to customize assessment features to meet the needs of every assignment.

B Your comments help you remember why you arrived at a rating and give you a starting point for discussing the assignment with the student or family.

C When desired, the rating may be turned into a letter grade.

Form for reproduction is on page129.
Spanish form for reproduction is on page 155.

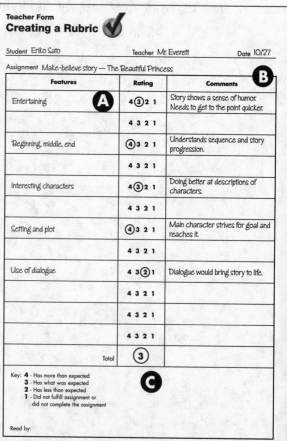

Teacher Form
Creating a Rubric

Student Eriko Sato   Teacher Mr. Everett   Date 10/27

Assignment Make-believe story — The Beautiful Princess

Features	Rating	Comments
Entertaining	4 ③ 2 1	Story shows a sense of humor. Needs to get to the point quicker.
	4 3 2 1	
Beginning, middle, end	④ 3 2 1	Understands sequence and story progression.
	4 3 2 1	
Interesting characters	4 ③ 2 1	Doing better at descriptions of characters.
	4 3 2 1	
Setting and plot	④ 3 2 1	Main character strives for goal and reaches it.
	4 3 2 1	
Use of dialogue	4 3 ② 1	Dialogue would bring story to life.
	4 3 2 1	
	4 3 2 1	
	4 3 2 1	
Total	③	

Key: **4** - Has more than expected
3 - Has what was expected
2 - Has less than expected
1 - Did not fulfill assignment or did not complete the assignment

Read by:

Grading Writing ✓

Grading Responses to Writing Prompts

- Writing prompts occur in several places in *Scott Foresman Reading Street*:

  – Following each selection and in the end-of-unit writing-process activity in the teacher's guide

  – In the Unit Benchmark Tests and the End-of-Year Benchmark Tests

- To grade students's writing, you can use the Creating a Rubric form. For your convenience, an example scale for a how-to response has been completed for you below. Actual determinations about what score equals which grade will, however, vary with different teachers and districts.

A List the features of a how-to article and add your own criteria if you wish.

B Comments help you remember why you arrived at a rating and give you a starting point for discussing the writing with the student.

C To determine the possible score, multiply the number of features by 4 (4 features x 4 = 16). Then add the ratings you've given the features to find the student's actual score. In this example 14 out of 16 = B.

Score	Grade
18–20	A
15–17	B
12–14	C
10–11	D
9 and below	F

Teacher Form
Creating a Rubric ✓

Student _Sandi Johnson_   Teacher _Miss Becht_   Date _3/16_

Assignment _How-to Article_

A Features	Rating	Comments
Tells what will be explained	④3 2 1	Good title and introduction
Steps in logical order	4 ③2 1	Needs to use time-order words to signal steps
Lists materials	4 ③2 1	Only if they're needed
Explains steps	④3 2 1	Lots of nice details
Correct grammar, punctuation and spelling	4 ③2 1	Only one careless error—handwriting
	4 3 2 1	
	4 3 2 1	
	4 3 2 1	
	4 3 2 1	
	4 3 2 1	
	4 3 2 1	
	4 3 2 1	
C Total	⑰	

Key: **4** - Has more than expected
   3 - Has what was expected
   2 - Has less than expected
   1 - Did not fulfill assignment or did not complete the assignment

Overall Grade
Ⓑ

Read by:

Form for reproduction is on page 129.
Spanish form for reproduction is on page155.

Grading Products and Activities

Grading Products and Activities

- The Creating a Rubric form lends itself to grading a variety of students' products and activities, including:
  - Class discussions
  - Speeches
  - Retellings
  - Oral readings and dramatizations
  - Drawings, sculptures, and other artwork
  - Graphic organizers such as Venn diagrams, story maps, concept maps, and KWL charts

- Two examples and grading scales—for a class discussion and for a graphic organizer—are provided here. Actual determinations about what score equals which grade will, however, vary with different teachers and districts.

- In determining the criteria on which to evaluate students' work, you may find it helpful to refer to the various teacher summary reports described earlier or to the other checklists in this handbook.

A Example for a CLASS DISCUSSION

B To get a grade:
5 features x 4 = 20;
19 out of 20 = A.

Score	Grade
18–20	A
15–17	B
12–14	C
10–11	D
9 and below	F

A

Student Dawn Kolak   Teacher Miss Bolt   Date 5/10

Assignment Class Discussion

Features	Rating	Comments
Gave detailed, thoughtful answers	④ 3 2 1	Came prepared to discuss
Backed up opinions with fact	④ 3 2 1	Great!
Asked questions to clarify	4 ③ 2 1	A little quiet but improving
Was supportive of others' ideas and opinions	4 ③ 2 1	Needs to show more outward reactions
Connected text to self	④ 3 2 1	Good—related to a famiy experience
	4 3 2 1	
	4 3 2 1	
	4 3 2 1	
	4 3 2 1	
	4 3 2 1	
	4 3 2 1	
	4 3 2 1	
B Total	⑱	

Key: **4** - Has more than expected
3 - Has what was expected
2 - Has less than expected
1 - Did not fulfill assignment or did not complete the assignment

Overall Grade
Ⓐ

Read by:

C Example for a GRAPHIC ORGANIZER

D To determine a grade:
4 features x 4 = 16;
14 out of 16 = B.

Score	Grade
15–16	A
13–14	B
11–12	C
10	D
9 and below	F

Form for reproduction is on page 129.
Spanish form for reproduction is on page 155.

Teacher Form
Creating a Rubric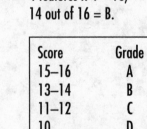

C

Student Laura Damon   Teacher Ms. Dolan   Date 11/3

Assignment Graphic Organizer

Features	Rating	Comments
Set up clear categories	4 3 ② 1	Categories were mixed between general & specific
Showed relationships between parts	4 ③ 2 1	Some relationships shown nicely
Included all important information	④ 3 2 1	Synthesized information very well
Was neat and well drawn	4 3 ② 1	Needs to work on presentation
	4 3 2 1	
	4 3 2 1	
	4 3 2 1	
	4 3 2 1	
	4 3 2 1	
	4 3 2 1	
	4 3 2 1	
	4 3 2 1	
D Total	⑪	

Key: **4** - Has more than expected
3 - Has what was expected
2 - Has less than expected
1 - Did not fulfill assignment or did not complete the assignment

Overall Grade
Ⓒ

Read by:

Grading Group Activities

**Grading Group
Activities**

- You can use the Creating a Rubric form to assign grades for group work. Students can be graded in one of two ways:
  - As group members working together
  - As individuals contributing to the group effort

- When evaluating the group as a unit, use criteria that emphasize students' ability to work together in an efficient and cooperative manner. Be mindful that cooperative or group grading can unfairly reward or penalize individual students.

- When assigning grades to individual students in a group, use criteria that emphasize the specific tasks the student must do. You might use students' reviews of their work on the group Assessment form described in chapter 3.

- The examples provided here show ways to evaluate and grade groups as well as individual students within groups. Actual determinations about what score equals which grade will vary with different teachers and districts.

A Example for a COOPERATIVE GROUP ACTIVITY

B These criteria assess students' ability to work together cooperatively and effectively.

C These criteria assess the actual product that students created.

D To get a grade:
6 features x 4 = 24;
22 out of 24 = A.

Score	Grade
15–16	A
13–14	B
11–12	C
10	D
9 and below	F

E Example for an INDIVIDUAL IN A GROUP

F These criteria assess individual students according to the specific tasks they have performed.

G To get a grade:
3 features x 4 = 12;
10 out of 12 = B.

Score	Grade
11–12	A
10	B
9	C
8	D
7 and below	F

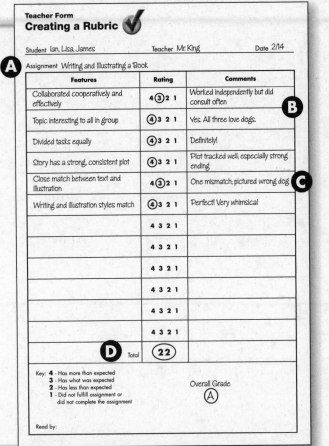

Teacher Form
Creating a Rubric ✓

Student Ian, Lisa, James   Teacher Mr. King   Date 2/14
Assignment Writing and Illustrating a Book

Features	Rating	Comments
Collaborated cooperatively and effectively	4 ③ 2 1	Worked independently but did consult often
Topic interesting to all in group	④ 3 2 1	Yes. All three love dogs.
Divided tasks equally	④ 3 2 1	Definitely!
Story has a strong, consistent plot	④ 3 2 1	Plot tracked well; especially strong ending
Close match between text and illustration	4 ③ 2 1	One mismatch; pictured wrong dog
Writing and illustration styles match	④ 3 2 1	Perfect! Very whimsical
	4 3 2 1	
	4 3 2 1	
	4 3 2 1	
	4 3 2 1	
	4 3 2 1	
	4 3 2 1	
Total	㉒	

Key: **4** - Has more than expected
3 - Has what was expected
2 - Has less than expected
1 - Did not fulfill assignment or did not complete the assignment

Overall Grade
Ⓐ

Read by:

Teacher Form
Creating a Rubric ✓

Student Ian Murphy   Teacher Mr. King   Date 2/14
Assignment Writing/Illustrating a Book

Features	Rating	Comments
Created half of book illustrations	④ 3 2 1	Worked conscientiously; finished ahead of schedule
Created illustrations that hit highlights of text	④ 3 2 1	Ian's illustrations were right on target.
Participated in development of story line	4 3 ② 1	Less attention to this than to doing the art
	4 3 2 1	
	4 3 2 1	
	4 3 2 1	
	4 3 2 1	
	4 3 2 1	
	4 3 2 1	
	4 3 2 1	
	4 3 2 1	
	4 3 2 1	
Total	⑩	

Key: **4** - Has more than expected
3 - Has what was expected
2 - Has less than expected
1 - Did not fulfill assignment or did not complete the assignment

Overall Grade
Ⓑ

Read by:

Form for reproduction is on page 129.
Spanish form for reproduction is on page 155.

Forms in English

Myself as a Reader and Writer

	A Lot	Sometimes	Not at All
Name Date			

1. I like to read

	A Lot	Sometimes	Not at All
realistic fiction	☐	☐	☐
fantasy stories (for example, tall tales, myths, science fiction)	☐	☐	☐
historical fiction	☐	☐	☐
plays	☐	☐	☐
biographies/autobiographies	☐	☐	☐
nonfiction articles	☐	☐	☐
other:	☐	☐	☐

2. The subjects I like to read about most are

	A Lot	Sometimes	Not at All
students my age	☐	☐	☐
sports	☐	☐	☐
famous people	☐	☐	☐
exploration and adventure	☐	☐	☐
how things work	☐	☐	☐
things that are funny	☐	☐	☐
other:	☐	☐	☐

3. I like to write

	A Lot	Sometimes	Not at All
made-up stories	☐	☐	☐
true stories	☐	☐	☐
letters	☐	☐	☐
poems	☐	☐	☐
reports	☐	☐	☐
plays	☐	☐	☐
other:	☐	☐	☐

4. The best book or story I have read in the last year is

_____

_____

5. The best thing I have written in the last year is a piece about

_____

_____

Name _____ Date _____

Mark the box next to the answer that tells how you feel.

1. How often do you like to read?

- ☐ All of the time
- ☐ Sometimes
- ☐ Not too often
- ☐ Never

2. When I read I

- ☐ always try my best.
- ☐ try my best most of the time.
- ☐ don't try very hard.
- ☐ often give up.

3. In general, when I read I

- ☐ really enjoy it.
- ☐ think it's OK.
- ☐ don't like it very much.
- ☐ dislike it a lot.

4. I think reading is

- ☐ my favorite thing to do.
- ☐ one of my favorite things to do.
- ☐ not one of my favorite things to do.
- ☐ my least favorite thing to do.

5. I read

- ☐ a lot better than my classmates.
- ☐ a little better than my classmates.
- ☐ about the same as my classmates.
- ☐ worse than my classmates.

6. When I am reading by myself, I understand

- ☐ most of what I read.
- ☐ some of what I read.
- ☐ not much of what I read.
- ☐ very little of what I read.

7. I am

- ☐ a great reader.
- ☐ a good reader.
- ☐ an OK reader.
- ☐ a poor reader.

8. I care what other kids think about my reading.

- ☐ never
- ☐ not too often
- ☐ sometimes
- ☐ always

9. I think that reading is

- ☐ very easy.
- ☐ kind of easy.
- ☐ kind of hard.
- ☐ very hard.

10. When I read in school I usually

- ☐ feel good about it.
- ☐ feel OK about it.
- ☐ feel not too good about it.
- ☐ feel terrible about it.

Mark the box next to the answer that tells how you feel.

11. I talk with my friends about the things that I read

- ☐ all of the time.
- ☐ sometimes.
- ☐ not too often.
- ☐ never.

12. People who read a lot are

- ☐ very interesting.
- ☐ kind of interesting.
- ☐ not very interesting.
- ☐ pretty boring.

13. I think that reading in school is

- ☐ very important.
- ☐ important.
- ☐ somewhat important.
- ☐ not too important.

14. I think that reading at home is

- ☐ very important.
- ☐ important.
- ☐ somewhat important.
- ☐ not too important.

15. I like getting a book for a present.

- ☐ all the time
- ☐ sometimes
- ☐ not very often
- ☐ never

16. I read newspapers

- ☐ very well.
- ☐ pretty well.
- ☐ not too well.
- ☐ not well at all.

17. I read schoolbooks

- ☐ very well.
- ☐ pretty well.
- ☐ not too well.
- ☐ not well at all.

18. I read comics

- ☐ very well.
- ☐ pretty well.
- ☐ not too well.
- ☐ not well at all.

19. I read magazines

- ☐ very well.
- ☐ pretty well.
- ☐ not too well.
- ☐ not well at all.

20. I read storybooks or novels

- ☐ very well.
- ☐ pretty well.
- ☐ not too well.
- ☐ not well at all.

Teacher Form

Profile of English Language Learners

Student:

Trait	Mostly	Unevenly	Rarely	Date/Comment
Oral Language				
Uses names of many objects				
Uses and understands basic everyday vocabulary				
Speaks hesitantly, searching for words				
Speaks fluently but makes errors				
Uses mostly present-tense verbs				
Has trouble with irregular forms (standed, more slower)				
Asks and answers simple questions				
Follows simple directions				
Is able to explain events or ideas				
Reading				
Recognizes basic sound/letter relationships in words				
Follows text being read aloud				
Needs pictures to comprehend text				

Teacher Form

Profile of English Language Learners (continued)

Student:

Trait	Mostly	Unevenly	Rarely	Date/Comment
Joins in choral reading				
Retells predictable text				
Recognizes many words by sight				
Relies on print more than on illustrations				
Retells beginning, middle, and end of things read				
Writing				
Writes labels for pictures of people and actions				
Uses single words or phrases to express ideas				
Writes simple but understandable sentences				
Spells simple words correctly				
Makes up spellings showing correct sound/letter relationships				
Uses standard word order				
Adds endings (-s, -es, 's, -s, -ed, -ing) correctly				
Understands basic capitalization and punctuation				
Writes sentences demonstrating fluency and control of vocabulary				

Name _____   Date _____

---

1. Which statement is most true about you?

a. ☐ I nearly always understand things better if I see a picture or diagram.

b. ☐ When someone explains something, I usually understand it just by listening.

c. ☐ Sometimes I need pictures to help me understand; other times I don't.

2. If you have a choice, you would rather work

a. ☐ in a group with three or four others

b. ☐ with one partner

c. ☐ by yourself

3. You want to remember a story you read. The best way for you to do this would be to

a. ☐ draw a picture of it

b. ☐ act out a scene from it

c. ☐ discuss it with a partner or group

d. ☐ do this instead:

_____

_____

4. You go to a museum. The kind of exhibit you like best has

a. ☐ a film to go with it

b. ☐ levers and buttons you can play with

c. ☐ a book where you can write what you liked and didn't like

d. ☐ something else:

_____

_____

5. Your group is planning a presentation about castles for younger students. The part you would like to do best is

a. ☐ design the invitations

b. ☐ build a model of the castle

c. ☐ talk to the students after the presentation to see how they liked it

d. ☐ something else:

_____

_____

Parent Form
My Child as a Learner

Name _____   Date _____

Please comment and provide examples of your child's learning in the following areas.			
My child	**Yes**	**No**	**Comments/Examples**
1. usually • reads daily • writes daily • watches TV daily	☐ ☐ ☐	☐ ☐ ☐	
2. often • is curious • persists with what s/he is doing • does things in new ways • becomes easily frustrated • likes trying new things • likes to express opinions	☐ ☐ ☐ ☐ ☐ ☐	☐ ☐ ☐ ☐ ☐ ☐	
3. understands what s/he is • reading • writing • watching	☐ ☐ ☐	☐ ☐ ☐	
4. explores ideas by • reading • writing • drawing • watching • talking	☐ ☐ ☐ ☐ ☐	☐ ☐ ☐ ☐ ☐	
5. enjoys working • with others • alone	☐ ☐	☐ ☐	
6. is someone who • is proud of achievement • recognizes own growth • considers new possibilities • sets goals for self	☐ ☐ ☐ ☐	☐ ☐ ☐ ☐	
7. likes to read about			
8. likes to write about			
9. likes to watch			
10. Additional comments and reactions:			
My name _____		Relationship to child _____	
I can be reached at			

Teacher Form

Narrative Retelling Chart

Selection Title _____

Name _____ Date _____

Retelling Criteria/Teacher Prompt	Teacher-Aided Response	Student-Generated Response	Rubric Score (Circle one.)			
Connections Has anything like this happened to you? How does this story remind you of other stories?			4	3	2	1
Author's Purpose Why do you think the author wrote this story? What was the author trying to tell us?			4	3	2	1
Characters Describe _____ (character's name) at the beginning and end of the story.			4	3	2	1
Setting Where and when did the story happen?			4	3	2	1
Plot Tell me what the story was about in a few sentences.			4	3	2	1

Summative Retelling Score   4   3   2   1

Comments _____

Teacher Form

Expository Retelling Chart

Selection Title _____ Name _____ Date _____

Retelling Criteria/Teacher Prompt	Teacher-Aided Response	Student-Generated Response	Rubric Score (Circle one.)			
Connections Did this selection make you think about something else you have read? What did you learn about as you read this selection?			4	3	2	1
Author's Purpose Why do you think the author wrote this selection?			4	3	2	1
Topic What was the selection mostly about?			4	3	2	1
Important Ideas What is important for me to know about _____ (topic)?			4	3	2	1
Conclusions What did you learn from reading this selection?			4	3	2	1

Summative Retelling Score 4 3 2 1

Comments _____

Teacher Form

Work Habits Conference Record

Student

Use the key at the bottom of the page to assess student's performance.

Date	Understands tasks	Sets priorities	Uses time appropriately	Solves problems effectively	Seeks help when needed	Completes tasks on time	Can explain process/ project effectively	Comments

4 Does more than expected   **3** Does what was expected   **2** Does less than expected   **1** Does not fulfill the assignment or does not complete the assignment

Teacher Form

Skills Conference Record

Grade _____

Student _____   Teacher _____

	Proficient	Developing	Having Difficulty	Not showing trait
Reading Comments:				
Sets own purpose for reading	☐	☐	☐	☐
Predicts and asks questions	☐	☐	☐	☐
Retells/Summarizes	☐	☐	☐	☐
Reads fluently	☐	☐	☐	☐
Understands key ideas in a text	☐	☐	☐	☐
Uses decoding strategies	☐	☐	☐	☐
Makes text connections	☐	☐	☐	☐
Other:	☐	☐	☐	☐
Writing Comments:				
Follows writing process	☐	☐	☐	☐
Develops main idea and supporting details	☐	☐	☐	☐
Organization of ideas	☐	☐	☐	☐
Writer's voice reveals purpose	☐	☐	☐	☐
Word choice expresses ideas	☐	☐	☐	☐
Varied sentence structure	☐	☐	☐	☐
Grammar and mechanics	☐	☐	☐	☐
Other:	☐	☐	☐	☐
Speaking and Listening Comments:				
Follows instructions	☐	☐	☐	☐
Asks questions	☐	☐	☐	☐
Answers questions	☐	☐	☐	☐
Paraphrases	☐	☐	☐	☐
Participates in discussions	☐	☐	☐	☐
Makes eye contact with audience	☐	☐	☐	☐
Other:	☐	☐	☐	☐

Teacher Form

Observing English Language Learners

Student:

Behaviors Observed	Date:			Date:			Date:			Date:		
	Yes	No	Sometimes	Yes	No	Sometimes	Yes	No	Sometimes	Yes	No	Sometimes
The student												
• uses context clues to figure out new words												
• uses prior knowledge to figure out new words												
• uses visuals to decipher meaning												
• uses strategies to decipher meaning												
• can identify the strategies he or she is using												
• understands why he or she is using a particular strategy												
• assesses his or her own progress												
• generally understands what the class is reading												

General Comments

Student Self-Assessment

Name _____ Teacher _____ Date _____

Work/Project I'm Assessing: _____

Things I Did Well	Things I Need to Work On
How I Will Work on Them	**My Goals for the Future**

Peer Assessment

My name is _____ Date_____

I'm looking at _____'s work.

The work I am looking at is _____.

Things I Especially Like About Your Work	Things I Had Trouble Understanding
_____	_____
_____	_____
_____	_____
_____	_____
_____	_____
_____	_____
_____	_____

Suggestions

_____

_____

_____

_____

_____

_____

_____

_____

Group Assessment

Teacher _____   Date _____

What the Group Did: _____

_____

_____

What I Did:

> **Member 1**
>
>
>
>
> **Member 2**
>
>
>
>
> **Member 3**
>
>
>
>
> **Member 4**

Problems We Had: _____

_____

_____

Our Goals for Next Time: _____

_____

Student Form

Reading Log

Name _____

Dates Read	Title and Author	What is it about?	How would you rate it?	Explain your rating.
From ___ to ___			**Great** 5 4 3 2 1 **Awful**	
From ___ to ___			**Great** 5 4 3 2 1 **Awful**	
From ___ to ___			**Great** 5 4 3 2 1 **Awful**	
From ___ to ___			**Great** 5 4 3 2 1 **Awful**	
From ___ to ___			**Great** 5 4 3 2 1 **Awful**	

About My Reading

Name _____   Date _____

---

1. **Compared with earlier in the year, I am enjoying reading**

   ☐ more   ☐ less   ☐ about the same

2. **When I read now, I understand**

   ☐ more than I used to   ☐ about the same as I used to

3. **One thing that has helped me with my reading is**

   _____

   _____

   _____

4. **One thing that could make me a better reader is**

   _____

   _____

   _____

5. **Here is one selection or book that I really enjoyed reading:**

   _____

   _____

6. **Here are some reasons why I liked it:**

   _____

   _____

   _____

   _____

   _____

   _____

Student Form

Writing Log

Student _____

Date _____

Teacher _____

Grade _____

Date	Title	Type of Writing	How I felt about this this piece	What I liked or disliked	Put in Portfolio
			4 3 2 1		
			4 3 2 1		
			4 3 2 1		
			4 3 2 1		
			4 3 2 1		
			4 3 2 1		

Key
4 = Excellent
3 = Good
2 = Fair
1 = Poor

About My Writing

Name   Date

1. Compared with earlier in the year, I am enjoying writing

☐ more   ☐ less   ☐ about the same

2. When I write now, my writing is

- clearer than it used to be   ☐ yes   ☐ no
- more interesting than it used to be   ☐ yes   ☐ no

3. One thing that has improved my writing is

_____

_____

_____

4. One thing that could make me a better writer is

_____

_____

_____

5. Here is one piece that I wrote that I think is really good:

_____

_____

6. Here are some things that are good about it:

_____

_____

_____

_____

_____

Name   Date   Grade

Form   **Date Submitted**

Knowledge About Books and Print   ☐

Reading Behaviors Checklist   ☐ ☐ ☐

Writing Behaviors Checklist   ☐ ☐ ☐

Oral Language Behaviors Checklist   ☐ ☐ ☐

Myself/My Child as a Learner   ☐

Other: _____   ☐

Record of Child's Work

Writers' Workshop Progress Chart   ☐

Selected Writing Piece   ☐ ☐ ☐ ☐ ☐ ☐

Unit 1 Benchmark Assessment Evaluation Chart   ☐

Unit 2 Benchmark Assessment Evaluation Chart   ☐

Unit 3 Benchmark Assessment Evaluation Chart   ☐

Unit 4 Benchmark Assessment Evaluation Chart   ☐

Unit 5 Benchmark Assessment Evaluation Chart   ☐

Unit 6 Benchmark Assessment Evaluation Chart   ☐

Other: _____   ☐

Other: _____   ☐

Other: _____   ☐

Other: _____   ☐

Name: _____

Date: _____

I chose this piece of work because

_____

_____

_____

_____

_____

_____

_____

Name: _____

Date: _____

I chose this piece of work because

_____

_____

_____

_____

_____

_____

_____

Name: _____

Date: _____

I chose this piece of work because

_____

_____

_____

_____

_____

_____

_____

Name: _____

Date: _____

I chose this piece of work because

_____

_____

_____

_____

_____

_____

_____

Teacher Form
Reading Strategy Assessment

Student _____ Date _____

Teacher _____ Grade _____

		Proficient	Developing	Emerging	Not showing trait
Building Background Comments:	Previews	☐	☐	☐	☐
	Ask questions	☐	☐	☐	☐
	Predicts	☐	☐	☐	☐
	Activates prior knowledge	☐	☐	☐	☐
	Sets own purposes for reading	☐	☐	☐	☐
	Other:	☐	☐	☐	☐
Comprehension Comments:	Retells/Summarizes	☐	☐	☐	☐
	Questions and evaluates ideas	☐	☐	☐	☐
	Paraphrases	☐	☐	☐	☐
	Rereads/reads ahead for meaning	☐	☐	☐	☐
	Visualizes	☐	☐	☐	☐
	Uses decoding strategies	☐	☐	☐	☐
	Uses vocabulary strategies	☐	☐	☐	☐
	Understands key ideas in a text	☐	☐	☐	☐
	Other:	☐	☐	☐	☐
Fluency Comments:	Adjusts reading rate	☐	☐	☐	☐
	Reads for accuracy	☐	☐	☐	☐
	Uses expression	☐	☐	☐	☐
	Other:	☐	☐	☐	☐
Connections Comments:	Relates text to text	☐	☐	☐	☐
	Relates text to self	☐	☐	☐	☐
	Relates text to world	☐	☐	☐	☐
	Other:	☐	☐	☐	☐
Self-Assessment Comments:	Is aware of: Strengths	☐	☐	☐	☐
	Needs	☐	☐	☐	☐
	Improvement/Achievement	☐	☐	☐	☐
	Sets and implements learning goals	☐	☐	☐	☐
	Maintains logs, records, portfolio	☐	☐	☐	☐
	Works with others	☐	☐	☐	☐
	Shares ideas and materials	☐	☐	☐	☐
	Other:	☐	☐	☐	☐

Teacher Form
Writing Strategy Assessment

Student _____ Date _____

Teacher _____ Grade _____

		Competent	Developing	Emerging	Not showing trait
Ideas Comments:	Identifies purpose in opening paragraph	☐	☐	☐	☐
	States main idea	☐	☐	☐	☐
	Details support main idea	☐	☐	☐	☐
	Gathers ideas and information	☐	☐	☐	☐
	Conclusion reinforces main idea	☐	☐	☐	☐
	Other:	☐	☐	☐	☐
Organization Comments:	Product of writing process	☐	☐	☐	☐
	Has a clear beginning, middle, and end	☐	☐	☐	☐
	Begins with a topic sentence	☐	☐	☐	☐
	Uses transitions between sentences and paragraphs	☐	☐	☐	☐
	Uses order words *(first, then, after, finally)*	☐	☐	☐	☐
	Other:	☐	☐	☐	☐
Voice Comments:	Speaks directly to audience	☐	☐	☐	☐
	Voice matches writer's purpose	☐	☐	☐	☐
	Shows rather than tells	☐	☐	☐	☐
	Writer's feelings and personality emerge	☐	☐	☐	☐
	Keeps reader's attention	☐	☐	☐	☐
	Other:	☐	☐	☐	☐
Word Choice Comments:	Uses vivid words to elaborate ideas	☐	☐	☐	☐
	Avoids slang and jargon	☐	☐	☐	☐
	Uses strong images or figurative language	☐	☐	☐	☐
	Uses action verbs versus linking verbs	☐	☐	☐	☐
	Uses new words to express ideas	☐	☐	☐	☐
	Other:	☐	☐	☐	☐
Sentence Fluency Comments:	Expresses thoughts in lively, varied sentences	☐	☐	☐	☐
	Mixes short and long sentences	☐	☐	☐	☐
	Includes questions, commands, and exclamations	☐	☐	☐	☐
	Sentences flow logically from one to another	☐	☐	☐	☐
	Avoids choppy and wordy sentences	☐	☐	☐	☐
	Other:	☐	☐	☐	☐
Conventions Comments:	Subjects and verbs are in agreement	☐	☐	☐	☐
	Uses correct punctuation for grade level	☐	☐	☐	☐
	Capitalizes proper nouns and sentence beginnings	☐	☐	☐	☐
	Forms plurals of nouns	☐	☐	☐	☐
	Words are spelled correctly	☐	☐	☐	☐
	Other:	☐	☐	☐	☐

© Pearson Education

Teacher Form

Cumulative Folder Form

Student _____   School _____

Group Placement Key: SI = Strategic Intervention   OL = On-Level   A = Advanced

Benchmark Test

Grade 3	Unit 1	Unit 2	Unit 3	Unit 4	Unit 5	Unit 6	End of Year
Comprehension	%	%	%	%	%	%	%
Vocabulary	%	%	%	%	%	%	%
Phonics	%	%	%	%	%	%	%
Grammar, Usage, Mechanics	%	%	%	%	%	%	%
Writing							
Fluency	wcpm	wcpm	wcpm	wcpm	wcpm	wcpm	wcpm
Group Placement							
Baseline Test							

Total Score: _____   Group Placement: _____

Additional Comments: _____

Teacher Signature: _____

Baseline Test Comments: _____

End-of-Year Date: _____

Group Placement Key: SI = Strategic Intervention   OL = On-Level   A = Advanced

Benchmark Test

Grade 4	Unit 1	Unit 2	Unit 3	Unit 4	Unit 5	Unit 6	End of Year
Comprehension	%	%	%	%	%	%	%
Vocabulary	%	%	%	%	%	%	%
Phonics	%	%	%	%	%	%	%
Grammar, Usage, Mechanics	%	%	%	%	%	%	%
Writing							
Fluency	wcpm	wcpm	wcpm	wcpm	wcpm	wcpm	wcpm
Group Placement							
Baseline Test							

Total Score: _____   Group Placement: _____

Additional Comments: _____

Teacher Signature: _____

Baseline Test Comments: _____

End-of-Year Date: _____

127

Teacher Form
Cumulative Folder Form

Student _____ School _____

Benchmark Assessment Test

Group Placement Key: SI = Strategic Intervention OL = On-Level A = Advanced

Grade 5	Unit 1	Unit 2	Unit 3	Unit 4	Unit 5	Unit 6	End of Year
Comprehension	%	%	%	%	%	%	%
Vocabulary	%	%	%	%	%	%	%
Phonics	%	%	%	%	%	%	%
Grammar, Usage, Mechanics	%	%	%	%	%	%	%
Writing							
Fluency	wcpm	wcpm	wcpm	wcpm	wcpm	wcpm	wcpm
Group Placement							
Baseline Test							

Total Score: _____ Group Placement: _____

Baseline Test Comments: _____

Additional Comments: _____

Teacher Signature: _____ End-of-Year Date: _____

Benchmark Test

Group Placement Key: SI = Strategic Intervention OL = On-Level A = Advanced

Grade 6	Unit 1	Unit 2	Unit 3	Unit 4	Unit 5	Unit 6	End of Year
Comprehension	%	%	%	%	%	%	%
Vocabulary	%	%	%	%	%	%	%
Phonics	%	%	%	%	%	%	%
Grammar, Usage, Mechanics	%	%	%	%	%	%	%
Writing							
Fluency	wcpm	wcpm	wcpm	wcpm	wcpm	wcpm	wcpm
Group Placement							
Baseline Test							

Total Score: _____ Group Placement: _____

Baseline Test Comments: _____

Additional Comments: _____

Teacher Signature: _____ End-of-Year Date: _____

Creating a Rubric ✔

Student _____   Teacher _____   Date _____

Assignment _____

Features	Rating	Comments
	4 3 2 1	
	4 3 2 1	
	4 3 2 1	
	4 3 2 1	
	4 3 2 1	
	4 3 2 1	
	4 3 2 1	
	4 3 2 1	
	4 3 2 1	
	4 3 2 1	
	4 3 2 1	
	4 3 2 1	
Total		

Key: **4** - Has more than expected
     3 - Has what was expected
     2 - Has less than expected
     1 - Did not fulfill assignment or
          did not complete the assignment

Read by: _____

Forms in Spanish

Formulario del estudiante

Yo, como lector y escritor

	Mucho	A veces	En absoluto
Nombre _____ Fecha _____			

1. Me gusta leer

	Mucho	A veces	En absoluto
ficción realista	☐	☐	☐
cuentos fantásticos (por ejemplo: cuentos exagerados, mitos, ciencia ficción)	☐	☐	☐
ficción histórica	☐	☐	☐
obras de teatro	☐	☐	☐
biografías / autobiografías	☐	☐	☐
artículos verídicos	☐	☐	☐
otros:	☐	☐	☐

2. Me gusta leer sobre

	Mucho	A veces	En absoluto
estudiantes de mi edad	☐	☐	☐
deportes	☐	☐	☐
gente famosa	☐	☐	☐
exploración y aventuras	☐	☐	☐
funcionamiento de las cosas	☐	☐	☐
cosas divertidas	☐	☐	☐
otros:	☐	☐	

3. Me gusta escribir

	Mucho	A veces	En absoluto
cuentos inventados	☐	☐	☐
historias reales	☐	☐	☐
cartas	☐	☐	☐
poemas	☐	☐	☐
informes	☐	☐	☐
obras de teatro	☐	☐	☐
otros:	☐	☐	☐

4. El mejor libro o cuento que he leído durante el último año es

_____

_____

5. Lo mejor que he escrito durante el último año es un texto sobre

_____

_____

Formulario del estudiante
La lectura y yo

Nombre   Fecha

Marca la respuesta más apropiada

1. ¿Cada cuánto te gusta leer?

- [ ] Todo el tiempo
- [ ] Algunas veces
- [ ] No muy a menudo
- [ ] Nunca

2. Cuando leo

- [ ] siempre intento hacerlo lo mejor posible.
- [ ] intento hacerlo lo mejor posible la mayoría de las veces.
- [ ] no me esfuerzo demasiado.
- [ ] a menudo me doy por vencido.

3. En general, cuando leo

- [ ] me encanta.
- [ ] me gusta.
- [ ] no me gusta demasiado.
- [ ] no me gusta nada.

4. Creo que leer

- [ ] es mi actividad favorita.
- [ ] es una de mis actividades favoritas.
- [ ] no es una de mis actividades favoritas.
- [ ] es la actividad que menos me gusta.

5. Leo

- [ ] mucho mejor que mis compañeros de clase.
- [ ] un poco mejor que mis compañeros de clase.
- [ ] más o menos igual que mis compañeros de clase.
- [ ] peor que mis compañeros de clase.

6. Cuando leo solo, entiendo

- [ ] la mayoría de lo que leo.
- [ ] parte de lo que leo.
- [ ] no mucho de lo que leo.
- [ ] muy poco de lo que leo.

7. Soy

- [ ] un excelente lector.
- [ ] un buen lector.
- [ ] un lector regular.
- [ ] un lector mediocre.

8. Me importa lo que piensan otros niños sobre mi lectura

- [ ] Nunca
- [ ] No muchas veces
- [ ] Algunas veces
- [ ] Siempre

9. En mi opinión leer es

- [ ] muy fácil.
- [ ] bastante fácil.
- [ ] bastante difícil.
- [ ] muy difícil.

10. Cuando leo en la escuela

- [ ] me siento satisfecho.
- [ ] me siento regular.
- [ ] no me siento muy satisfecho.
- [ ] me siento fatal.

Marca la respuesta más apropiada

11. Hablo con mis amigos sobre lo que leo

☐ todo el tiempo.
☐ a veces.
☐ no muy a menudo.
☐ nunca.

12. Las personas que leen mucho son

☐ muy interesantes.
☐ bastante interesantes.
☐ no muy interesantes.
☐ bastante aburridas.

13. Creo que leer en la escuela es

☐ muy importante.
☐ importante.
☐ un poco importante.
☐ no muy importante.

14. Creo que leer en casa es

☐ muy importante.
☐ importante.
☐ un poco importante.
☐ no muy importante.

15. Me gusta recibir un libro como regalo

☐ todo el tiempo.
☐ a veces.
☐ no muy a menudo.
☐ nunca.

16. Leo periódicos

☐ muy bien.
☐ bastante bien.
☐ no muy bien.
☐ nada bien.

17. Leo libros de la escuela

☐ muy bien.
☐ bastante bien.
☐ no muy bien.
☐ nada bien.

18. Leo tiras cómicas

☐ muy bien.
☐ bastante bien.
☐ no muy bien.
☐ nada bien.

19. Leo revistas

☐ muy bien.
☐ bastante bien.
☐ no muy bien.
☐ nada bien.

20. Leo libros de cuentos o novelas

☐ muy bien.
☐ bastante bien.
☐ no muy bien.
☐ nada bien.

© Pearson Education

Formulario del maestro

Perfil de los estudiantes de inglés como segundo idioma

Estudiante:

Característica	Generalmente	De forma irregular	Raramente	Fecha/Comentario
Lenguaje oral				
Usa nombres de muchos objetos				
Emplea y comprende el vocabulario diario básico				
Habla con indecisión, buscando palabras				
Habla con fluidez, pero comete errores				
Emplea mayoritariamente verbos en el presente				
Muestra dificultades con las formas irregulares (por ejemplo: abrido, más menor)				
Formula y contesta preguntas sencillas				
Sigue instrucciones sencillas				
Es capaz de explicar sucesos o ideas				
Lectura				
Reconoce la relación básica entre sonidos y letras en las palabras				
Sigue un texto leído en voz alta				
Necesita ilustraciones para comprender el texto				

Perfil de los estudiantes de inglés como segundo idioma (continuación)

Estudiante:

Característica	Generalamente	De forma irregular	Raramente	Fecha/Comentario
Participa en la lectura en coro				
Vuelve a contar un texto predecible				
Reconoce muchas palabras a simple vista				
Se basa en el texto más que en las ilustraciones				
Vuelve a contar el principio, el medio y el final de lo leído				
Escritura				
Escribe rótulos para dibujos de personas y acciones				
Emplea palabras individuales o frases para expresar ideas				
Escribe oraciones sencillas pero con sentido				
Deletrea palabras sencillas correctamente				
Intenta deletrear las palabras, identificando correctamente los sonidos con las letras correspondientes				
Usa el orden estándar de las palabras				
Añade terminaciones (-s, -es, -ces, -ando,-iendo, -ado, -ido) correctamente				
Comprende el uso de las mayúsculas y la puntuación				
Escribe oraciones demostrando fluidez y buen manejo del vocabulario				

¿Cómo aprendo?

Nombre   Fecha

1. ¿Cuál de estas afirmaciones se ajusta más a tu realidad?

a. ☐ Casi siempre entiendo mejor las cosas si veo una ilustración o un diagrama.

b. ☐ Cuando alguien explica algo, generalmente lo entiendo tan sólo escuchando.

c. ☐ Algunas veces necesito ilustraciones para entender mejor; otras veces no.

2. Si puedes escoger, prefieres trabajar

a. ☐ en grupo con otras tres o cuatro personas.

b. ☐ con un compañero.

c. ☐ tú solo.

3. Quieres acordarte de un cuento que has leído. Prefieres

a. ☐ hacer un dibujo.

b. ☐ representar una escena del cuento.

c. ☐ comentarlo con un compañero o en clase.

d. ☐ hacer lo siguiente:

_____

_____

4. Vas a un museo. La exposición que más te gusta

a. ☐ va acompañada por una película.

b. ☐ tiene palancas y botones para jugar.

c. ☐ tiene un libro donde se puede escribir lo que te gustó y no te gustó.

d. ☐ tiene otra cosa:

_____

_____

5. Tu clase está planeando una presentación sobre castillos para unos estudiantes más jóvenes. Prefieres

a. ☐ diseñar las invitaciones.

b. ☐ construir un modelo del castillo.

c. ☐ hablar con los estudiantes después de la presentación para que comenten si les gustó.

d. ☐ otra cosa:

_____

_____

Formulario de los padres
Mi hijo(a) como estudiante

Nombre   Fecha

Por favor comenten y proporcionen ejemplos sobre el aprendizaje de su hijo(a) en las siguientes áreas.			
Mi hijo	**Sí**	**No**	**Comentarios/Ejemplos**
1. por lo general • lee a diario • escribe a diario • ve la televisión a diario	☐ ☐ ☐	☐ ☐ ☐	
2. a menudo • es curioso • persiste en lo que está haciendo • renueva la forma de hacer las cosas • se frustra con facilidad • le gusta intentar cosas nuevas • le gusta expresar opiniones	☐ ☐ ☐ ☐ ☐ ☐	☐ ☐ ☐ ☐ ☐ ☐	
3. entiende lo que está • leyendo • escribiendo • viendo	☐ ☐ ☐	☐ ☐ ☐	
4. explora ideas • leyendo • escribiendo • dibujando • observando • hablando	☐ ☐ ☐ ☐ ☐	☐ ☐ ☐ ☐ ☐	
5. disfruta al trabajar • con otros • solo	☐ ☐	☐ ☐	
6. es una persona que • se enorgullece de sus logros • reconoce su propio crecimiento • considera nuevas posibilidades • se impone objetivos	☐ ☐ ☐ ☐	☐ ☐ ☐ ☐	
7. disfruta leer sobre			
8. disfruta escribir sobre			
9. disfruta ver			
10. Comentarios adicionales y reacciones:			
Mi nombre Relación con el(la) niño(a)			
Se me puede localizar en			

Formulario del maestro

Tabla para volver a contar un texto narrativo

Título de la obra _____ Nombre _____ Fecha _____

Criterios para volver a contar/Apunte del maestro	Respuesta con la ayuda del maestro	Respuesta del niño	Evaluación (Encierre uno en un círculo.)			
Conexiones ¿Te ha pasado algo parecido? ¿En qué sentido te recuerda este cuento de otros cuentos?			4	3	2	1
La intención del autor ¿Por qué crees que el autor escribió este cuento? ¿Qué nos estaba intentando decir el autor?			4	3	2	1
Personajes Describe _____ (el nombre del personaje) al principio y al final del cuento?			4	3	2	1
Escenario ¿Dónde y cuándo tuvo lugar el cuento?			4	3	2	1
Argumento ¿En unas frases, dime de qué se trataba el cuento?			4	3	2	1

Evaluación acumulativa 4 3 2 1

Comentarios _____

139

Formulario del maestro

Tabla para volver a contar un texto expositivo

Título de la obra _____ Nombre _____ Fecha _____

Criterios para volver a contar/Apunte del maestro	Respuesta con la ayuda del maestro	Respuesta del estudiante	Evaluación (Encierre uno en un círculo.)			
Conexiones ¿Esta obra te hizo pensar en otra cosa ques has leído? ¿Qué has aprendido mientras leías esta obra?			4	3	2	1
La intención del autor ¿Por qué crees que el autor escribió esta obra?			4	3	2	1
Tema ¿De que se trataba en general esta obra?			4	3	2	1
Ideas importantes Para mi, ¿qué es importante saber sobre _____ (tema)?			4	3	2	1
Conclusiones ¿Qué aprendiste al leer esta obra?			4	3	2	1

Evaluación acumulativa 4 3 2 1

Comentarios _____

Formulario del maestro
Anotaciones de la conferencia sobre el rendimiento en los estudios

Estudiante _____

Use la guía para calificar del final de la página, para evaluar el rendimiento del estudiante.

Fecha	Comprende las tareas	Establece prioridades	Emplea el tiempo adecuadamente	Resuelve problemas eficazmente	Pide ayuda cuando la necesita	Termina las tareas a tiempo	Puede explicar el proceso/proyecto eficazmente	Comments

4 Independiente   **3** Con un poco de ayuda   **2** Con ayuda frecuente   **1** No se observó

Anotaciones de la conferencia sobre el desarollo de las destrezas

Grado _____

Estudiante _____   Maestro _____

		competente	en vías de desarrollo	con dificultad	No muestra la característica
Lectura Comentarios:	Establece su propia razón para leer	☐	☐	☐	☐
	Predice y hace preguntas	☐	☐	☐	☐
	Vuelve a contar/Resume	☐	☐	☐	☐
	Lee con fluidez	☐	☐	☐	☐
	Comprende las ideas clave de un texto	☐	☐	☐	☐
	Usa estrategias para descifrar	☐	☐	☐	☐
	Hace conexiones con del texto	☐	☐	☐	☐
	Otros:	☐	☐	☐	☐
Escritura Comentarios:	Sigue el proceso de escribir	☐	☐	☐	☐
	Desarrolla la idea principal y los detalles que la apoya	☐	☐	☐	☐
	Organización de ideas	☐	☐	☐	☐
	La voz del escritor identifica su intención	☐	☐	☐	☐
	Las palabras escogidas expresan ideas	☐	☐	☐	☐
	Hay variedad en la estructura de las frases	☐	☐	☐	☐
	Gramática y ortografía y puntuación	☐	☐	☐	☐
	Otros:	☐	☐	☐	☐
Hablar y escuchar Comentarios:	Sigue instrucciones	☐	☐	☐	☐
	Hace preguntas	☐	☐	☐	☐
	Contesta preguntas	☐	☐	☐	☐
	Parafrasear	☐	☐	☐	☐
	Hablar sobre temas	☐	☐	☐	☐
	Mantiene contacto visual con los oyentes	☐	☐	☐	☐
	Otros:	☐	☐	☐	☐

Formulario del maestro

Observar a los estudiantes de inglés como segundo idioma

Estudiante:

Comportamientos observados	Fecha:			Fecha:			Fecha:			Fecha:		
	Sí	No	A veces	Sí	No	A veces	Sí	No	A veces	Sí	No	A veces
El estudiante												
• usa claves de contexto para determinar el significado de las palabras nuevas												
• usa conocimientos previos para determinar el significado de las palabras nuevas												
• usa recursos visuales para descifrar el significado												
• usa estrategias para descifrar el significado												
• sabe identificar las estrategias que usa												
• comprende por qué usa una estrategia en particular												
• evalúa su propio progreso												
• en general comprende lo que la clase está leyendo												
Comentarios generales												

Autoevaluación del estudiante ✓

Nombre _____ Maestro _____ Fecha _____

Tarea/proyecto que estoy evaluando: _____

Cosas que hice bien	Cosas que tengo que mejorar

Cómo voy a mejorarlas	Mis objetivos en el futuro

Evaluación de los compañeros

Me llamo _____ Fecha _____

Estoy viendo el trabajo de _____.

El trabajo que estoy viendo se llama _____.

Cosas que me gustan en especial sobre tu trabajo	**Cosas que me resultaron difíciles de entender**

Sugerencias

Evaluación en grupo ✓

Maestro _____   Fecha _____

Lo que el grupo hizo: _____

_____

_____

Lo que yo hice:

Miembro 1
Miembro 2
Miembro 3
Miembro 4

Problemas que tuvimos: _____

_____

_____

Nuestros objetivos para la próxima vez: _____

_____

Formulario del estudiante
Diario de lectura

Nombre _____

Fechas de lectura	Título y autor	¿De qué se trata?	¿Cómo lo calificarías?	Explica tu calificación.
De ___ a ___			**Estupendo** **Terrible** 5 4 3 2 1	
De ___ a ___			**Estupendo** **Terrible** 5 4 3 2 1	
De ___ a ___			**Estupendo** **Terrible** 5 4 3 2 1	
De ___ a ___			**Estupendo** **Terrible** 5 4 3 2 1	
De ___ a ___			**Estupendo** **Terrible** 5 4 3 2 1	

Nombre _____   Date _____

1. **Me gusta leer** _____ **que al principio del año.**

   ☐ **más**   ☐ **menos**   ☑ **más o menos igual**

2. **Cuando leo entiendo**

   ☐ **más que antes.**   ☐ **aproximadamente igual que antes.**

3. _____

   _____

   _____ **me ha ayudado a leer mejor.**

4. _____

   _____

   _____ **me ayudaría a ser un mejor lector.**

5. **La selección o libro que me encantó leer se llama:**

   _____

   _____

6. **Algunas razones por las que me gustó son:**

   _____

   _____

   _____

   _____

   _____

   _____

Formulario del estudiante
Diario de escritura

Estudiante _____

Maestro _____

Fecha _____

Grado _____

Fecha	Título	Tipo de escritura	Lo qué opiné de este trabajo	Lo que me gustó o no me gustó	En el portafolios
			4 3 2 1		
			4 3 2 1		
			4 3 2 1		
			4 3 2 1		
			4 3 2 1		
			4 3 2 1		

Clave
4 = Excelente
3 = Bueno
2 = Mediocre
1 = Pobre

Nombre _____   Fecha _____

1. Me gusta escribir _____ que al principio del año.

☐ más   ☐ menos   ☐ más o menos igual

2. Cuando escribo, mi trabajo es

• **más claro que antes**   ☐ sí   ☐ no

• **más interesante que antes**   ☐ sí   ☐ no

3. _____

_____

_____ **me ha ayudado a mejorar mi escritura.**

4. _____

_____

_____ **me ayudaría a ser un mejor escritor.**

5. Este texto que escribí es, en mi opinión, muy bueno:

_____

_____

6. Algunas cosas buenas sobre el texto son:

_____

_____

_____

_____

Guía del portafolios ✓

Grado

Nombre

Fecha

Formulario

Fecha entregado

Conocimientos de libros y la palabra escrita ☐

Lista para evaluar el progreso en la lectura ☐ ☐ ☐

Lista para evaluar el progreso en la escritura ☐ ☐ ☐

Lista para evaluar el progreso en el lenguaje oral ☐ ☐ ☐

Yo/Mi hijo(a) como estudiante ☐

Otros: _____ ☐

Documentos sobre el trabajo del estudiante

Tabla de progreso del taller de escritores ☐

Trabajo escrito seleccionado ☐ ☐ ☐ ☐ ☐ ☐

Unidad 1 Tabla de evaluación para el examen de progreso ☐

Unidad 2 Tabla de evaluación para el examen de progreso ☐

Unidad 3 Tabla de evaluación para el examen de progreso ☐

Unidad 4 Tabla de evaluación para el examen de progreso ☐

Unidad 5 Tabla de evaluación para el examen de progreso ☐

Unidad 6 Tabla de evaluación para el examen de progreso ☐

Otros: _____ ☐

Otros: _____ ☐

Otros: _____ ☐

Otros: _____ ☐

Papelitos de selecciones para el portafolios

Nombre: _____

Fecha: _____

Escogí este trabajo porque

_____

_____

_____

_____

_____

_____

_____

Nombre: _____

Fecha: _____

Escogí este trabajo porque

_____

_____

_____

_____

_____

_____

_____

Nombre: _____

Fecha: _____

Escogí este trabajo porque

_____

_____

_____

_____

_____

_____

_____

Nombre: _____

Fecha: _____

Escogí este trabajo porque

_____

_____

_____

_____

_____

_____

_____

Evaluación de estrategias en la lectura

Estudiante _____ Fecha _____

Maestro _____ Grado _____

		Competente	En vías de desarrollo	Principiante	No muestra la característica
Formación Comentarios:	Anticipa	☐	☐	☐	☐
	Hace preguntas	☐	☐	☐	☐
	Predice	☐	☐	☐	☐
	Utiliza conocimientos anteriores	☐	☐	☐	☐
	Establece sus propias razones para leer	☐	☐	☐	☐
	Otros:	☐	☐	☐	☐
Comprensión Comentarios:	Vuelve a contar/Resume	☐	☐	☐	☐
	Duda y evalúa ideas	☐	☐	☐	☐
	Parafrasea	☐	☐	☐	☐
	Lee otra vez/se adelanta en la lectura para captar el significado	☐	☐	☐	☐
	Visualiza	☐	☐	☐	☐
	Usa estrategias para descifrar	☐	☐	☐	☐
	Usa estrategias para vocabulario	☐	☐	☐	☐
	Comprende las ideas clave de un texto	☐	☐	☐	☐
	Otros:				
Fluidez Comentarios:	Ajusta la velocidad con que lee	☐	☐	☐	☐
	Lee con precisión	☐	☐	☐	☐
	Es expresivo	☐	☐	☐	☐
	Otros:	☐	☐	☐	☐
Conexiones Comentarios:	Relaciona el texto con el texto	☐	☐	☐	☐
	Relaciona el texto consigo mismo	☐	☐	☐	☐
	Relaciona el texto con el mundo	☐	☐	☐	☐
	Otros:	☐	☐	☐	☐
Autoevaluación Comentarios:	Se da cuenta de: sus fuerzas	☐	☐	☐	☐
	sus necesidades	☐	☐	☐	☐
	su mejoría/sus logros	☐	☐	☐	☐
	Establece y pone en práctica sus objetivos didácticos	☐	☐	☐	☐
	Mantiene diarios, documentos, portafolios	☐	☐	☐	☐
	Trabaja con otros	☐	☐	☐	☐
	Comparte ideas y materiales	☐	☐	☐	☐
	Otros:	☐	☐	☐	☐

Formulario del maestro
Evaluación de estrategias en la escritura

Estudiante _____ Fecha _____

Maestro _____ Grado _____

		Competente	En vías de desarrollo	Principiante	No muestra la característica
Ideas Comentarios:	Identifica el propósito en el primer párrafo	☐	☐	☐	☐
	Expone la idea principal	☐	☐	☐	☐
	Los detalles apoyan la idea principal	☐	☐	☐	☐
	Junta ideas e información	☐	☐	☐	☐
	La conclusión reafirma la idea principal	☐	☐	☐	☐
	Otros:	☐	☐	☐	☐
Organización Comentarios:	Producto del proceso de escribir	☐	☐	☐	☐
	Tiene un principio, medio y final claros	☐	☐	☐	☐
	Comienza con una frase que expone la idea principal	☐	☐		
	Usa transiciones entre las frases y los párrafos	☐	☐	☐	☐
	Usa palabras que muestran secuencia *(primero luego, después, por fin)*	☐	☐		☐
	Otros:	☐	☐		☐
Voz Comentarios:	Habla directamente al público	☐	☐	☐	☐
	La voz corresponde al propósito del escritor	☐	☐	☐	☐
	Muestra en vez de contar	☐	☐	☐	☐
	Se notan los sentimientos y el carácter del escritor	☐	☐	☐	☐
	Mantiene la atención del lector	☐	☐	☐	☐
	Otros:	☐	☐	☐	☐
Selección de palabras Comentarios:	Usa palabras vivas para elaborar ideas	☐	☐	☐	☐
	Evita el argot y la jerga	☐	☐	☐	☐
	Usa imágenes fuertes o lenguaje figurativo	☐	☐	☐	☐
	Usa verbos activos, no copulativos	☐	☐	☐	☐
	Usa palabras nuevas para expresar ideas	☐	☐	☐	☐
	Otros:	☐	☐	☐	☐
Fluidez de frases Comentarios:	Expresa sus pensamientos con frases variadas y vivas	☐	☐	☐	☐
	Hay una mezcla de frases largas y cortas	☐	☐	☐	☐
	Incluye preguntas, mandatos y exclamaciones	☐	☐	☐	☐
	Las frases fluyen lógicamente entre sí	☐	☐	☐	☐
	Evita frases desonantes y de demasiadas palabras	☐	☐	☐	☐
	Otros:	☐	☐	☐	☐
Normas Comentarios:	Los sujetos y los verbos concuerdan	☐	☐	☐	☐
	Usa correctamente la puntuación, según el grado	☐	☐	☐	☐
	Usa letras mayúsculas para los sustantivos propios y la primera palabra de una frase	☐	☐		
	Forma los plurales de los sustantivos	☐	☐	☐	☐
	La ortografía es correcta	☐	☐	☐	☐
	Otros:	☐	☐	☐	☐

Crear una guía para calificar

Estudiante _____ Maestro _____ Fecha _____

Tarea

Características	Calificación	Comentarios
	4 3 2 1	
	4 3 2 1	
	4 3 2 1	
	4 3 2 1	
	4 3 2 1	
	4 3 2 1	
	4 3 2 1	
	4 3 2 1	
	4 3 2 1	
	4 3 2 1	
	4 3 2 1	
	4 3 2 1	
Total		

Guía: **4** - Más de lo esperado
3 - Lo que se esperaba
2 - Menos de lo esperado
1 - No realizó la tarea o no terminó la tarea

Leído por:

Assessment and Regrouping Charts for Grade 3

From *Scott Foresman Reading Street* Teacher's Editions

Fluency Progress Chart, Grade 3

	1	2	3	4	5	6	7	8	9	10	11	12	13	14	15	16	17	18	19	20	21	22	23	24	25	26	27	28	29	30
145																														
140																														
135																														
130																														
125																														
120																														
115																														
110																														
105																														
100																														
95																														
90																														
85																														
80																														
75																														
70																														
65																														
60																														
55																														
50																														

Timed Reading

Assessment and Regrouping Chart

Unit 1

© Pearson Education

	Day 3 Retelling Assessment		Day 5 Fluency Assessment		Reteach	Teacher's Comments	Grouping
	The assessed group is highlighted for each week.		The assessed group is highlighted for each week.		✓		
	Benchmark Score	Actual Score	Benchmark WCPM	Actual Score			
WEEK 1 **Boom Town** Realism and Fantasy							
Strategic	1–2		Less than 80				
On-Level	3		80–90				
Advanced	4		80–90				
WEEK 2 **What About Me?** Sequence							
Strategic	1–2		Less than 80				
On-Level	3		80–90				
Advanced	4		Advanced*				
WEEK 3 **Alexander Who Used to Be Rich Last Sunday** Sequence							
Strategic	1–2		Less than 80				
On-Level	3		80–90				
Advanced	4		Advanced*				
WEEK 4 **If You Made a Million** Realism and Fantasy							
Strategic	1–2		Less than 80				
On-Level	3		80–90				
Advanced	4		Advanced*				
WEEK 5 **My Rows and Piles of Coins** Character and Setting							
Strategic	1–2		Less than 80				
On-Level	3		80–90				
Advanced	4		Advanced*				
Unit 1 Benchmark Test Score							

* **RECORD SCORES** Use this chart to record scores for the Day 3 Retelling, Day 5 Fluency, and Unit 1 Benchmark Test Assessments.

*Students in the advanced group should read above grade-level materials.

* **REGROUPING** Compare the student's actual score to the benchmark score for each group level and review the Questions to Consider. Students may move to a higher or lower group level, or they may remain in the same group.

* **RETEACH** If a student is unable to complete any part of the assessment process, use the weekly Reteach lessons for additional support. Record the lesson information in the space provided on the chart. After reteaching, you may want to reassess using the Unit Benchmark Test.

© Pearson Education

Grade 3, Unit 1, Page 147k

Assessment and Regrouping Chart

	Day 3 Retelling Assessment		Day 5 Fluency Assessment		Reteach	Teacher's Comments	Grouping
The assessed group is highlighted for each week.	Benchmark Score	Actual Score	The assessed group is highlighted for each week.	Benchmark WCPM	Actual Score			
WEEK 1 **Penguin Chick** Main Idea and Details					✓		
Strategic	1–2		Strategic	Less than 85			
On-Level	3		On-Level	85–95			
Advanced	4		Advanced*	85–95			
WEEK 2 **A Day's Work** Character							
Strategic	1–2		Strategic	Less than 85			
On-Level	3		On-Level	85–95			
Advanced	4		Advanced*	85–95			
WEEK 3 **Prudy's Problem** Main Idea							
Strategic	1–2		Strategic	Less than 85			
On-Level	3		On-Level	85–95			
Advanced	4		Advanced*	85–95			
WEEK 4 **Tops & Bottoms** Author's Purpose							
Strategic	1–2		Strategic	Less than 85			
On-Level	3		On-Level	85–95			
Advanced	4		Advanced*	85–95			
WEEK 5 **William's House** Draw Conclusions							
Strategic	1–2		Strategic	Less than 85			
On-Level	3		On-Level	85–95			
Advanced	4		Advanced*	85–95			
Unit 2 Benchmark Test Score							

- **RECORD SCORES** Use this chart to record scores for the Day 3 Retelling, Day 5 Fluency, and Unit Benchmark Test Assessments.

*Students in the advanced group should read above grade-level materials.

- **REGROUPING** Compare the student's actual score to the benchmark score for each group level and review the Questions to Consider. Students may move to a higher or lower group level, or they may remain in the same group.

- **RETEACH** If a student is unable to complete any part of the assessment process, use the weekly Reteach lessons for additional support. Record the lesson information in the space provided on the chart. After reteaching, you may want to reassess using the Unit Benchmark Test.

Grade 3, Unit 2, Page 277k

Name _____   Date _____

Assessment and Regrouping Chart   Unit 3

	Day 3 Retelling Assessment		Day 5 Fluency Assessment		Reteach	Teacher's Comments	Grouping
The assessed group is highlighted for each week.	Benchmark Score	Actual Score	Benchmark WCPM	Actual Score *The assessed group is highlighted for each week.*			
WEEK 1 *The Gardener* Cause and Effect					✓		
Strategic	1–2		Less than 90	Strategic			
On-Level	3		90–100	On-Level			
Advanced	4		90–100	Advanced*			
WEEK 2 *Pushing Up the Sky* Author's Purpose							
Strategic	1–2		Less than 90	Strategic			
On-Level	3		90–100	On-Level			
Advanced	4		90–100	Advanced*			
WEEK 3 *Night Letters* Draw Conclusions							
Strategic	1–2		Less than 90	Strategic			
On-Level	3		90–100	On-Level			
Advanced	4		90–100	Advanced*			
WEEK 4 *A Symphony of Whales* Generalize							
Strategic	1–2		Less than 90	Strategic			
On-Level	3		90–100	On-Level			
Advanced	4		90–100	Advanced*			
WEEK 5 *Volcanoes: Nature's Incredible Fireworks* Compare and Contrast							
Strategic	1–2		Less than 90	Strategic			
On-Level	3		90–100	On-Level			
Advanced	4		90–100	Advanced*			
Unit 3 Benchmark Test Score							

- **RECORD SCORES** Use this chart to record scores for the Day 3 Retelling, Day 5 Fluency, and Unit Benchmark Test Assessments.

*Students in the advanced group should read above grade-level materials.

- **REGROUPING** Compare the student's actual score to the benchmark score for each group level and review the Questions to Consider. Students may move to a higher or lower group level, or they may remain in the same group.

- **RETEACH** If a student is unable to complete any part of the assessment process, use the weekly Reteach lessons for additional support. Record the lesson information in the space provided on the chart. After reteaching, you may want to reassess using the Unit Benchmark Test.

Grade 3, Unit 3, Page 405k

Assessment and Regrouping Chart

Unit 4

	Day 3 Retelling Assessment			Day 5 Fluency Assessment			Reteach	Teacher's Comments	Grouping
	The assessed group is highlighted for each week.	Benchmark Score	Actual Score	The assessed group is highlighted for each week.	Benchmark WCPM	Actual Score			
WEEK 1 — *Wings* Cause and Effect	Strategic	1–2		Strategic	Less than 95		✓		
	On-Level	3		On-Level	95–105				
	Advanced	4		Advanced*	95–105				
WEEK 2 — *Hottest, Coldest, Highest, Deepest* Compare and Contrast	Strategic	1–2		Strategic	Less than 95				
	On-Level	3		On-Level	95–105				
	Advanced	4		Advanced*	95–105				
WEEK 3 — *Rocks in His Head* Generalize	Strategic	1–2		Strategic	Less than 95				
	On-Level	3		On-Level	95–105				
	Advanced	4		Advanced*	95–105				
WEEK 4 — *America's Champion Swimmer: Gertrude Ederle* Fact and Opinion	Strategic	1–2		Strategic	Less than 95				
	On-Level	3		On-Level	95–105				
	Advanced	4		Advanced*	95–105				
WEEK 5 — *Fly, Eagle, Fly!* Plot and Theme	Strategic	1–2		Strategic	Less than 95				
	On-Level	3		On-Level	95–105				
	Advanced	4		Advanced*	95–105				
Unit 4 Benchmark Test Score									

*Students in the advanced group should read above grade-level materials.

- **RECORD SCORES** Use this chart to record scores for the Day 3 Retelling, Day 5 Fluency, and Unit Benchmark Test Assessments.

- **REGROUPING** Compare the student's actual score to the benchmark score for each group level and review the Questions to Consider. Students may move to a higher or lower group level, or they may remain in the same group.

- **RETEACH** If a student is unable to complete any part of the assessment process, use the weekly Reteach lessons for additional support. Record the lesson information in the space provided on the chart. After reteaching, you may want to reassess using the Unit Benchmark Test.

© Pearson Education

Name _____ **Date** _____

Assessment and Regrouping Chart

Unit 5

	Day 3 Retelling Assessment		Day 5 Fluency Assessment		Reteach	Teacher's Comments	Grouping
	The assessed group is highlighted for each week.		The assessed group is highlighted for each week.				
	Benchmark Score	Actual Score	Benchmark WCPM	Actual Score			
WEEK 1 **Suki's Kimono** Compare and Contrast					✓		
Strategic	1–2		Less than 102				
On-Level	3		102–112				
Advanced	4		102–112				
WEEK 2 **How My Family Lives in America** Fact and Opinion							
Strategic	1–2		Less than 102				
On-Level	3		102–112				
Advanced	4		102–112				
WEEK 3 **Good-Bye 382 Shin Dang Dong** Sequence							
Strategic	1–2		Less than 102				
On-Level	3		102–112				
Advanced	4		102–112				
WEEK 4 **Jalapeño Bagels** Draw Conclusions							
Strategic	1–2		Less than 102				
On-Level	3		102–112				
Advanced	4		102–112				
WEEK 5 **Me and Uncle Romie** Author's Purpose							
Strategic	1–2		Less than 102				
On-Level	3		102–112				
Advanced	4		102–112				
Unit 5 Benchmark Test Score							

*Students in the advanced group should read above grade-level materials.

- **RECORD SCORES** Use this chart to record scores for the Day 3 Retelling, Day 5 Fluency, and Unit Benchmark Test Assessments.

- **REGROUPING** Compare the student's actual score to the benchmark score for each group level and review the Questions to Consider. Students may move to a higher or lower group level, or they may remain in the same group.

- **RETEACH** If a student is unable to complete any part of the assessment process, use the weekly Reteach lessons for additional support. Record the lesson information in the space provided on the chart. After reteaching, you may want to reassess using the Unit Benchmark Test.

Grade 3, Unit 5, Page 281k

Assessment and Regrouping Chart

	Day 3 Retelling Assessment		Day 5 Fluency Assessment		Reteach	Teacher's Comments	Grouping
The assessed group is highlighted for each week.	Benchmark Score	Actual Score	Benchmark WCPM	Actual Score			
			The assessed group is highlighted for each week.				
WEEK 1 — *The Story of the Statue of Liberty* — Main Idea and Details					✓		
Strategic	1–2		Less than 110				
On-Level	3		110–120				
Advanced	4		110–120				
WEEK 2 — *Happy Birthday Mr. Kang* — Cause and Effect							
Strategic	1–2		Less than 110				
On-Level	3		110–120				
Advanced	4		110–120				
WEEK 3 — *Talking Walls: Art for the People* — Fact and Opinion							
Strategic	1–2		Less than 110				
On-Level	3		110–120				
Advanced	4		110–120				
WEEK 4 — *Two Bad Ants* — Plot and Theme							
Strategic	1–2		Less than 110				
On-Level	3		110–120				
Advanced	4		110–120				
WEEK 5 — *Elena's Serenade* — Generalize							
Strategic	1–2		Less than 110				
On-Level	3		110–120				
Advanced	4		110–120				
Unit 6 Benchmark Test Score							

- **RECORD SCORES** Use this chart to record scores for the Day 3 Retelling, Day 5 Fluency, and Unit Benchmark Test Assessments.

*Students in the advanced group should read above grade-level materials.

- **REGROUPING** Compare the student's actual score to the benchmark score for each group level and review the Questions to Consider. Students may move to a higher or lower group level, or they may remain in the same group.

- **RETEACH** If a student is unable to complete any part of the assessment process, use the weekly Reteach lessons for additional support. Record the lesson information in the space provided on the chart. After reteaching, you may want to reassess using the Unit Benchmark Test.

Assessment and Regrouping Charts for Grade 4

From *Scott Foresman Reading Street* Teacher's Editions

Fluency Progress Chart, Grade 4

Name _____

	165	160	155	150	145	140	135	130	125	120	115	110	105	100	95	90	85	80	75	70

| 1 | 2 | 3 | 4 | 5 | 6 | 7 | 8 | 9 | 10 | 11 | 12 | 13 | 14 | 15 | 16 | 17 | 18 | 19 | 20 | 21 | 22 | 23 | 24 | 25 | 26 | 27 | 28 | 29 | 30 |

Timed Reading

Grade 4, Unit 1, Page 139j

Name _____ Date _____

Assessment and Regrouping Chart

Unit 1

	Day 3 Retelling Assessment			Day 5 Fluency Assessment			Reteach	Teacher's Comments	Grouping
The assessed group is highlighted for each week.		Benchmark Score	Actual Score	The assessed group is highlighted for each week.	Benchmark WCPM	Actual Score	✓		
WEEK 1 **Because of Winn-Dixie** Sequence	Strategic	1–2		Strategic	Less than 95				
	On-Level	3		On-Level	95–105				
	Advanced	4		Advanced*	95–105				
WEEK 2 **Lewis and Clark and Me** Author's Purpose	Strategic	1–2		Strategic	Less than 95				
	On-Level	3		On-Level	95–105				
	Advanced	4		Advanced*	95–105				
WEEK 3 **Grandfather's Journey** Sequence	Strategic	1–2		Strategic	Less than 95				
	On-Level	3		On-Level	95–105				
	Advanced	4		Advanced*	95–105				
WEEK 4 **The Horned Toad Prince** Author's Purpose	Strategic	1–2		Strategic	Less than 95				
	On-Level	3		On-Level	95–105				
	Advanced	4		Advanced*	95–105				
WEEK 5 **Letters Home** Main Idea	Strategic	1–2		Strategic	Less than 95				
	On-Level	3		On-Level	95–105				
	Advanced	4		Advanced*	95–105				

Unit 1 Benchmark Test Score

- **RECORD SCORES** Use this chart to record scores for the Day 3 Retelling, Day 5 Fluency, and Unit 1 Benchmark Test Assessments.

*Students in the advanced group should read above-grade-level materials.

- **RE-GROUPING** Compare the student's actual score to the benchmark score for each group level and review the *Questions to Consider*. Students may move to a higher or lower group level, or they may remain in the same group.

- **RETEACH** If a student is unable to complete any part of the assessment process, use the weekly Reteach lessons for additional support. Record the lesson information in the space provided on the chart. After reteaching, you may want to reassess using the Unit Benchmark Test.

Grade 4, Unit 1, Page 139k

Assessment and Regrouping Chart
Unit 2

	Day 3 Retelling Assessment		Day 5 Fluency Assessment		Reteach	Teacher's Comments	Grouping
The assessed group is highlighted for each week.	Benchmark Score	Actual Score	Benchmark WCPM	Actual Score	✓		
WEEK 1 **What Jo Did** Cause/Effect							
Strategic	1–2		Less than 100				
On-Level	3		100–110				
Advanced	4		100–110				
WEEK 2 **Coyote School News** Draw Conclusions							
Strategic	1–2		Less than 100				
On-Level	3		100–110				
Advanced	4		100–110				
WEEK 3 **Grace** Draw Conclusions							
Strategic	1–2		Less than 100				
On-Level	3		100–110				
Advanced	4		100–110				
WEEK 4 **Marven** Fact/Opinion							
Strategic	1–2		Less than 100				
On-Level	3		100–110				
Advanced	4		100–110				
WEEK 5 **Want to Be President?** Main Idea							
Strategic	1–2		Less than 100				
On-Level	3		100–110				
Advanced	4		100–110				
Unit 2 Benchmark Test Score							

*Students in the advanced group should read above-grade-level materials.

- **RECORD SCORES** Use this chart to record scores for the Day 3 Retelling, Day 5 Fluency, and Unit Benchmark Test Assessments.

- **RE-GROUPING** Compare the student's actual score to the benchmark score for each group level and review the *Questions to Consider*. Students may move to a higher or lower group level, or they may remain in the same group.

- **RETEACH** If a student is unable to complete any part of the assessment process, use the weekly Reteach lessons for additional support. Record the lesson information in the space provided on the chart. After reteaching, you may want to reassess using the Unit Benchmark Test.

Name _____ **Date** _____

Assessment and Regrouping Chart

Unit 3

	Day 3 Retelling Assessment		Day 5 Fluency Assessment		Reteach	Teacher's Comments	Grouping
The assessed group is highlighted for each week.	Benchmark Score	Actual Score	*The assessed group is highlighted for each week.*	Benchmark WCPM	Actual Score			
WEEK 1 — *The Stranger* Cause/Effect								
Strategic	1–2		Strategic	Less than 105		✓		
On-Level	3		On-Level	105–115				
Advanced	4		Advanced*	105–115				
WEEK 2 — *Adelina's Whales* Fact/Opinion								
Strategic	1–2		Strategic	Less than 105				
On-Level	3		On-Level	105–115				
Advanced	4		Advanced*	105–115				
WEEK 3 — *How Night Came* Generalize								
Strategic	1–2		Strategic	Less than 105				
On-Level	3		On-Level	105–115				
Advanced	4		Advanced*	105–115				
WEEK 4 — *Eye of the Storm* Graphic Sources								
Strategic	1–2		Strategic	Less than 105				
On-Level	3		On-Level	105–115				
Advanced	4		Advanced*	105–115				
WEEK 5 — *The Great Kapok Tree* Generalize								
Strategic	1–2		Strategic	Less than 105				
On-Level	3		On-Level	105–115				
Advanced	4		Advanced*	105–115				
Unit 3 Benchmark Test Score								

- **RECORD SCORES** Use this chart to record scores for the Day 3 Retelling, Day 5 Fluency, and Unit Benchmark Test Assessments.

  *Students in the advanced group should read above-grade-level materials.

- **RE-GROUPING** Compare the student's actual score to the benchmark score for each group level and review the *Questions to Consider*. Students may move to a higher or lower group level, or they may remain in the same group.

- **RETEACH** If a student is unable to complete any part of the assessment process, use the weekly Reteach lessons for additional support. Record the lesson information in the space provided on the chart. After reteaching, you may want to reassess using the Unit Benchmark Test.

Assessment and Regrouping Chart   Unit 4

The assessed group is highlighted for each week.	Day 3 Retelling Assessment		Day 5 Fluency Assessment		Reteach	Teacher's Comments	Grouping
	Benchmark Score	Actual Score	Benchmark WCPM	Actual Score			
WEEK 1 — *The Houdini Box* Compare/Contrast	Strategic **1–2**		Strategic Less than 110		✓		
	On-Level **3**		On-Level 110–120				
	Advanced **4**		Advanced* 110–120				
WEEK 2 — *Encantado* Compare/Contrast	Strategic **1–2**		Strategic Less than 110				
	On-Level **3**		On-Level 110–120				
	Advanced **4**		Advanced* 110–120				
WEEK 3 — *King in the Kitchen* Character/Setting	Strategic **1–2**		Strategic Less than 110				
	On-Level **3**		On-Level 110–120				
	Advanced **4**		Advanced* 110–120				
WEEK 4 — *Seeker of Knowledge* Graphic Sources	Strategic **1–2**		Strategic Less than 110				
	On-Level **3**		On-Level 110–120				
	Advanced **4**		Advanced* 110–120				
WEEK 5 — *Encyclopedia Brown* Plot	Strategic **1–2**		Strategic Less than 110				
	On-Level **3**		On-Level 110–120				
	Advanced **4**		Advanced* 110–120				
Unit 4 Benchmark Test Score							

*Students in the advanced group should read above-grade-level materials.

- **RECORD SCORES** Use this chart to record scores for the Day 3 Retelling, Day 5 Fluency, and Unit Benchmark Test Assessments.

- **RE-GROUPING** Compare the student's actual score to the benchmark score for each group level and review the *Questions to Consider*. Students may move to a higher or lower group level, or they may remain in the same group.

- **RETEACH** If a student is unable to complete any part of the assessment process, use the weekly Reteach lessons for additional support. Record the lesson information in the space provided on the chart. After reteaching, you may want to reassess using the Unit Benchmark Test.

© Pearson Education

Grade 4, Unit 4, Page 513k

Name _____ **Date** _____

Assessment and Regrouping Chart

Unit 5

	Day 3 Retelling Assessment *The assessed group is highlighted for each week.*		Day 5 Fluency Assessment *The assessed group is highlighted for each week.*		Reteach	Teacher's Comments	Grouping
	Benchmark Score	Actual Score	Benchmark WCPM	Actual Score			
WEEK 1 **Sailing Home** Author's Purpose					✓		
Strategic	1–2		Strategic — Less than 115				
On-Level	3		On-Level — 115–125				
Advanced	4		Advanced* — 115–125				
WEEK 2 **Lost City** Compare/Contrast							
Strategic	1–2		Strategic — Less than 115				
On-Level	3		On-Level — 115–125				
Advanced	4		Advanced* — 115–125				
WEEK 3 **Amelia and Eleanor** Sequence							
Strategic	1–2		Strategic — Less than 115				
On-Level	3		On-Level — 115–125				
Advanced	4		Advanced* — 115–125				
WEEK 4 **Antarctic Journal** Main Idea							
Strategic	1–2		Strategic — Less than 115				
On-Level	3		On-Level — 115–125				
Advanced	4		Advanced* — 115–125				
WEEK 5 **"Moonwalk"** Draw Conclusions							
Strategic	1–2		Strategic — Less than 115				
On-Level	3		On-Level — 115–125				
Advanced	4		Advanced* — 115–125				
Unit 5 Benchmark Test Score							

- **RECORD SCORES** Use this chart to record scores for the Day 3 Retelling, Day 5 Fluency, and Unit Benchmark Test Assessments.

*Students in the advanced group should read above-grade-level materials.

- **RE-GROUPING** Compare the student's actual score to the benchmark score for each group level and review the *Questions to Consider.* Students may move to a higher or lower group level, or they may remain in the same group.

- **RETEACH** If a student is unable to complete any part of the assessment process, use the weekly Reteach lessons for additional support. Record the lesson information in the space provided on the chart. After reteaching, you may want to reassess using the Unit Benchmark Test.

Grade 4, Unit 5, Page 635k

Assessment and Regrouping Chart   Unit 6

	Day 3 Retelling Assessment		Day 5 Fluency Assessment		Reteach	Teacher's Comments	Grouping
The assessed group is highlighted for each week.	Benchmark Score	Actual Score	Benchmark WCPM	Actual Score			
The assessed group is highlighted for each week.					✓		
WEEK 1 — *My Brother Martin* — Cause/Effect							
Strategic	1–2		Less than 120				
On-Level	3		120–130				
Advanced	4		120–130				
WEEK 2 — *Jim Thorpe's Path* — Fact/Opinion							
Strategic	1–2		Less than 120				
On-Level	3		120–130				
Advanced	4		120–130				
WEEK 3 — *Tía Lola* — Character/Theme							
Strategic	1–2		Less than 120				
On-Level	3		120–130				
Advanced	4		120–130				
WEEK 4 — *To Fly* — Generalize							
Strategic	1–2		Less than 120				
On-Level	3		120–130				
Advanced	4		120–130				
WEEK 5 — *Far Side of the Moon* — Graphic Sources							
Strategic	1–2		Less than 120				
On-Level	3		120–130				
Advanced	4		120–130				
Unit 6 Benchmark Test Score							

* **RECORD SCORES** Use this chart to record scores for the Day 3 Retelling, Day 5 Fluency, and Unit 6 Benchmark Test Assessments.

*Students in the advanced group should read above-grade-level materials.

* **RE-GROUPING** Compare the student's actual score to the benchmark score for each group level and review the *Questions to Consider*. Students may move to a higher or lower group level, or they may remain in the same group.

* **RETEACH** If a student is unable to complete any part of the assessment process, use the weekly Reteach lessons for additional support. Record the lesson information in the space provided on the chart. After reteaching, you may want to reassess using the Unit Benchmark Test.

Assessment and Regrouping Charts for Grade 5

From *Scott Foresman Reading Street* Teacher's Editions

Fluency Progress Chart, Grade 5

Name _____

	1	2	3	4	5	6	7	8	9	10	11	12	13	14	15	16	17	18	19	20	21	22	23	24	25	26	27	28	29	30
175																														
170																														
165																														
160																														
155																														
150																														
145																														
140																														
135																														
130																														
125																														
120																														
115																														
110																														
105																														
100																														
95																														
90																														
85																														
80																														

Timed Reading

Grade 5, Unit 1, Page 139j

Name _____

Date _____

Assessment and Regrouping Chart

Unit 1

	Day 3 Retelling Assessment		Day 5 Fluency Assessment			Reteach	Teacher's Comments	Grouping
	The assessed group is highlighted for each week.		*The assessed group is highlighted for each week.*					
	Benchmark Score	Actual Score	Benchmark wcPM		Actual Score			
WEEK 1 **Frindle** Character and Plot	1–2		Strategic	Less than 105		✓		
	3		On-Level	105–110				
	4		Advanced*	105–110				
WEEK 2 **Thunder Rose** Cause and Effect	1–2		Strategic	Less than 105				
	3		On-Level	105–110				
	4		Advanced*	105–110				
WEEK 3 **Island of Blue Dolphins** Setting and Theme	1–2		Strategic	Less than 105				
	3		On-Level	105–110				
	4		Advanced*	105–110				
WEEK 4 **Satchel Paige** Sequence	1–2		Strategic	Less than 105				
	3		On-Level	105–110				
	4		Advanced*	105–110				
WEEK 5 **Shutting Out the Sky** Cause and Effect	1–2		Strategic	Less than 105				
	3		On-Level	105–110				
	4		Advanced*	105–110				
Unit 4 Benchmark Test Score								

*Students in the advanced group should read above-grade-level materials.

- **RECORD SCORES** Use this chart to record scores for the Day 3 Retelling, Day 5 Fluency, and Unit Benchmark Test Assessments.

- **REGROUPING** Compare the student's actual score to the benchmark score for each group level and review the *Questions to Consider*. Students may move to a higher or lower group level, or they may remain in the same group.

- **RETEACH** If a student is unable to complete any part of the assessment process, use the weekly Reteach lessons for additional support. Record the lesson information in the space provided on the chart. After reteaching, you may want to reassess using the Unit Benchmark Test.

Grade 5, Unit 1, Page 139k

Assessment and Regrouping Chart

Unit 2

	Day 3 Retelling Assessment		Day 5 Fluency Assessment		Reteach	Teacher's Comments	Grouping
The assessed group is highlighted for each week.	Benchmark Score	Actual Score	*The assessed group is highlighted for each week.*	Benchmark WCPM	Actual Score			
WEEK 1 — *Inside Out* — Compare and Contrast					✓		
Strategic	1–2		Strategic	Less than 110				
On-Level	3		On-Level	110–116				
Advanced	4		Advanced*	110–116				
WEEK 2 — *Passage to Freedom* — Author's Purpose							
Strategic	1–2		Strategic	Less than 110				
On-Level	3		On-Level	110–116				
Advanced	4		Advanced*	110–116				
WEEK 3 — *The Ch'i-lin Purse* — Compare and Contrast							
Strategic	1–2		Strategic	Less than 110				
On-Level	3		On-Level	110–116				
Advanced	4		Advanced*	110–116				
WEEK 4 — *Jane Goodall's 10 Ways* — Fact and Opinion							
Strategic	1–2		Strategic	Less than 110				
On-Level	3		On-Level	110–116				
Advanced	4		Advanced*	110–116				
WEEK 5 — *The Midnight Ride* — Sequence							
Strategic	1–2		Strategic	Less than 110				
On-Level	3		On-Level	110–116				
Advanced	4		Advanced*	110–116				
Unit 2 Benchmark Test Score							

• **RECORD SCORES** Use this chart to record scores for the Day 3 Retelling, Day 5 Fluency, and Unit Benchmark Test Assessments.

*Students in the advanced group should read above-grade-level materials.

• **REGROUPING** Compare the student's actual score to the benchmark score for each group level and review the *Questions to Consider.* Students may move to a higher or lower group level, or they may remain in the same group.

• **RETEACH** If a student is unable to complete any part of the assessment process, use the weekly Reteach lessons for additional support. Record the lesson information in the space provided on the chart. After reteaching, you may want to reassess using the Unit Benchmark Test.

© Pearson Education

Name _____

Assessment and Regrouping Chart

Date _____

Unit 3

	Day 3 Retelling Assessment			Day 5 Fluency Assessment		Reteach	Teacher's Comments	Grouping
The assessed group is highlighted for each week.	Benchmark Score	Actual Score	*The assessed group is highlighted for each week.*	Benchmark WCPM	Actual Score			
WEEK 1 — *Wings for the King* Author's Purpose	1–2 / Strategic		Strategic	Less than 115		✓		
	3 / On-Level		On-Level	115–122				
	4 / Advanced		Advanced*	115–122				
WEEK 2 — *Leonardo's Horse* Main Idea	1–2 / Strategic		Strategic	Less than 115				
	3 / On-Level		On-Level	115–122				
	4 / Advanced		Advanced*	115–122				
WEEK 3 — *Dinosaurs of Waterhouse* Fact and Opinion	1–2 / Strategic		Strategic	Less than 115				
	3 / On-Level		On-Level	115–122				
	4 / Advanced		Advanced*	115–122				
WEEK 4 — *Mahalia Jackson* Main Idea	1–2 / Strategic		Strategic	Less than 115				
	3 / On-Level		On-Level	115–122				
	4 / Advanced		Advanced*	115–122				
WEEK 5 — *Special Effects* Graphic Sources	1–2 / Strategic		Strategic	Less than 115				
	3 / On-Level		On-Level	115–122				
	4 / Advanced		Advanced*	115–122				
Unit 3 Benchmark Test Score								

*Students in the advanced group should read above-grade-level materials.

- **RECORD SCORES** Use this chart to record scores for the Day 3 Retelling, Day 5 Fluency, and Unit Benchmark Test Assessments.

- **REGROUPING** Compare the student's actual score to the benchmark score for each group level and review the *Questions to Consider*. Students may move to a higher or lower group level, or they may remain in the same group.

- **RETEACH** If a student is unable to complete any part of the assessment process, use the weekly Reteach lessons for additional support. Record the lesson information in the space provided on the chart. After reteaching, you may want to reassess using the Unit Benchmark Test.

Grade 5, Unit 3, Page 389k

Assessment and Regrouping Chart   Unit 4

	Day 3 Retelling Assessment		Day 5 Fluency Assessment		Reteach	Teacher's Comments	Grouping
The assessed group is highlighted for each week.	Benchmark Score	Actual Score	Benchmark wcpm	Actual Score			
WEEK 1 **Weslandia** Draw Conclusions					✓		
Strategic	1–2		Less than 120				
On-Level	3		120–128				
Advanced*	4		120–128				
WEEK 2 **Stretching Ourselves** Generalize							
Strategic	1–2		Less than 120				
On-Level	3		120–128				
Advanced*	4		120–128				
WEEK 3 **Exploding Ants** Graphic Sources							
Strategic	1–2		Less than 120				
On-Level	3		120–128				
Advanced*	4		120–128				
WEEK 4 **Stormi Giovanni Club** Generalize							
Strategic	1–2		Less than 120				
On-Level	3		120–128				
Advanced*	4		120–128				
WEEK 5 **The Gymnast** Draw Conclusions							
Strategic	1–2		Less than 120				
On-Level	3		120–128				
Advanced*	4		120–128				
Unit 4 Benchmark Test Score							

*Students in the advanced group should read above-grade-level materials.

- **RECORD SCORES** Use this chart to record scores for the Day 3 Retelling, Day 5 Fluency, and Unit 4 Benchmark Test Assessments.

- **RE-GROUPING** Compare the student's actual score to the benchmark score for each group level and review the *Questions to Consider*. Students may move to a higher or lower group level, or they may remain in the same group.

- **RETEACH** If a student is unable to complete any part of the assessment process, use the weekly Reteach lessons for additional support. Record the lesson information in the space provided on the chart. After reteaching, you may want to reassess using the Unit Benchmark Test.

© Pearson Education

Name _____   Date _____

Assessment and Regrouping Chart   Unit 5

Day 3 Retelling Assessment			Day 5 Fluency Assessment			Reteach	Teacher's Comments	Grouping
The assessed group is highlighted for each week.	Benchmark Score	Actual Score	The assessed group is highlighted for each week.	Benchmark WCPM	Actual Score	✓		
Three-Century Woman Character/Plot								
Strategic	1–2		Strategic	Less than 125				
On-Level	3		On-Level	125–134				
Advanced	4		Advanced*	125–134				
Wreck of the Titanic Graphic Sources								
Strategic	1–2		Strategic	Less than 125				
On-Level	3		On-Level	125–134				
Advanced	4		Advanced*	125–134				
Talk with an Astronaut Author's Purpose								
Strategic	1–2		Strategic	Less than 125				
On-Level	3		On-Level	125–134				
Advanced	4		Advanced*	125–134				
Journey to the Center Cause/Effect								
Strategic	1–2		Strategic	Less than 125				
On-Level	3		On-Level	125–134				
Advanced	4		Advanced*	125–134				
Ghost Towns Generalize								
Strategic	1–2		Strategic	Less than 125				
On-Level	3		On-Level	125–134				
Advanced	4		Advanced*	125–134				
Unit 5 Benchmark Test Score								

WEEK 1 WEEK 2 WEEK 3 WEEK 4 WEEK 5

- **RECORD SCORES** Use this chart to record scores for the Day 3 Retelling, Day 5 Fluency, and Unit Benchmark Test Assessments.

*Students in the advanced group should read above-grade-level materials.

- **RE-GROUPING** Compare the student's actual score to the benchmark score for each group level and review the *Questions to Consider*. Students may move to a higher or lower group level, or they may remain in the same group.

- **RETEACH** If a student is unable to complete any part of the assessment process, use the weekly Reteach lessons for additional support. Record the lesson information in the space provided on the chart. After reteaching, you may want to reassess using the Unit Benchmark Test.

Grade 5, Unit 5, Page 631k

Assessment and Regrouping Chart

Unit 6

	Day 3 Retelling Assessment			Day 5 Fluency Assessment			Reteach	Teacher's Comments	Grouping
The assessed group is highlighted for each week.	Benchmark Score	Actual Score		The assessed group is highlighted for each week.	Benchmark WCPM	Actual Score			
WEEK 1 **At the Beach** Draw Conclusions							✓		
Strategic	1–2			Strategic	Less than 130				
On-Level	3			On-Level	130–140				
Advanced	4			Advanced*	130–140				
WEEK 2 **Saint Matthew Island** Main Idea									
Strategic	1–2			Strategic	Less than 130				
On-Level	3			On-Level	130–140				
Advanced	4			Advanced*	130–140				
WEEK 3 **King Midas** Compare and Contrast									
Strategic	1–2			Strategic	Less than 130				
On-Level	3			On-Level	130–140				
Advanced	4			Advanced*	130–140				
WEEK 4 **The Hindenburg** Fact and Opinion									
Strategic	1–2			Strategic	Less than 130				
On-Level	3			On-Level	130–140				
Advanced	4			Advanced*	130–140				
WEEK 5 **Sweet Music In Harlem** Sequence									
Strategic	1–2			Strategic	Less than 130				
On-Level	3			On-Level	130–140				
Advanced	4			Advanced*	130–140				
Unit 6 Benchmark Test Score									

- **RECORD SCORES** Use this chart to record scores for the Day 3 Retelling, Day 5 Fluency, and Unit Benchmark Test Assessments.

*Students in the advanced group should read above-grade-level materials.

- **RE-GROUPING** Compare the student's actual score to the benchmark score for each group level and review the *Questions to Consider*. Students may move to a higher or lower group level, or they may remain in the same group.

- **RETEACH** If a student is unable to complete any part of the assessment process, use the weekly Reteach lessons for additional support. Record the lesson information in the space provided on the chart. After reteaching, you may want to reassess using the Unit Benchmark Test.

© Pearson Education

Assessment and Regrouping Charts for Grade 6

From *Scott Foresman Reading Street* Teacher's Editions

Fluency Progress Chart, Grade 6

Name _____

	1	2	3	4	5	6	7	8	9	10	11	12	13	14	15	16	17	18	19	20	21	22	23	24	25	26	27	28	29	30
180																														
175																														
170																														
165																														
160																														
155																														
150																														
145																														
140																														
135																														
130																														
125																														
120																														
115																														
110																														
105																														
100																														
95																														
90																														
85																														

Timed Reading

Grade 6, Unit 3, Page 405j

Name _____   **Date** _____

Assessment and Regrouping Chart   Unit 1

	Day 3 Retelling Assessment			**Day 5 Fluency Assessment**			**Reteach**	**Teacher's Comments**	**Grouping**
	The assessed group is highlighted for each week.	Benchmark Score	Actual Score	The assessed group is highlighted for each week.	Benchmark WCPM	Actual Score			
WEEK 1	**Old Yeller** Setting						✓		
	Strategic	1–2		Strategic	Less than 115				
	On-Level	3		On-Level	115–120				
	Advanced	4		Advanced*	115–120				
WEEK 2	**Mother Fletcher's Gift** Character								
	Strategic	1–2		Strategic	Less than 115				
	On-Level	3		On-Level	115–120				
	Advanced	4		Advanced*	115–120				
WEEK 3	**Viva New Jersey** Compare/Contrast								
	Strategic	1–2		Strategic	Less than 115				
	On-Level	3		On-Level	115–120				
	Advanced	4		Advanced*	115–120				
WEEK 4	**Saving the Rain Forests** Fact/Opinion								
	Strategic	1–2		Strategic	Less than 115				
	On-Level	3		On-Level	115–120				
	Advanced	4		Advanced*	115–120				
WEEK 5	**When Crowbar Came** Fact/Opinion								
	Strategic	1–2		Strategic	Less than 115				
	On-Level	3		On-Level	115–120				
	Advanced	4		Advanced*	115–120				
	Unit 1 Benchmark Test Score								

- **RECORD SCORES** Use this chart to record scores for the Day 3 Retelling, Day 5 Fluency, and Unit Benchmark Test Assessments.

*Students in the advanced group should read above-grade-level materials.

- **RE-GROUPING** Compare the student's actual score to the benchmark score for each group level and review the Questions to Consider. Students may move to a higher or lower group level, or they may remain in the same group.

- **RETEACH** If a student is unable to complete any part of the assessment process, use the weekly Reteach lessons for additional support. Record the lesson information in the space provided on the chart. After reteaching, you may want to reassess using the Unit Benchmark Test.

Grade 6, Unit 1, Page 143k

Assessment and Regrouping Chart

Unit 2

	Day 3 Retelling Assessment		Day 5 Fluency Assessment		Reteach	Teacher's Comments	Grouping
The assessed group is highlighted for each week.	Benchmark Score	Actual Score	*The assessed group is highlighted for each week.* Benchmark WCPM	Actual Score	✓		
WEEK 1 — **The Universe** Main Idea							
Strategic	1–2		Less than 120				
On-Level	3		120–126				
Advanced*	4		120–126				
WEEK 2 — **Dinosaur Ghosts** Main Idea							
Strategic	1–2		Less than 120				
On-Level	3		120–126				
Advanced*	4		120–126				
WEEK 3 — **A Week in the 1800s** Graphic Sources							
Strategic	1–2		Less than 120				
On-Level	3		120–126				
Advanced*	4		120–126				
WEEK 4 — **Good-bye to the Moon** Compare and Contrast							
Strategic	1–2		Less than 120				
On-Level	3		120–126				
Advanced*	4		120–126				
WEEK 5 — **Egypt** Graphic Sources							
Strategic	1–2		Less than 120				
On-Level	3		120–126				
Advanced*	4		120–126				
Unit 2 Benchmark Test Score							

*Students in the advanced group should read above-grade-level materials.

- **RECORD SCORES** Use this chart to record scores for the Day 3 Retelling, Day 5 Fluency, and Unit Benchmark Test Assessments.

- **RE-GROUPING** Compare the student's actual score to the benchmark score for each group level and review the *Questions to Consider*. Students may move to a higher or lower group level, or they may remain in the same group.

- **RETEACH** If a student is unable to complete any part of the assessment process, use the weekly Reteach lessons for additional support. Record the lesson information in the space provided on the chart. After reteaching, you may want to reassess using the Unit Benchmark Test.

© Pearson Education

Assessment and Regrouping Chart   Unit 3

	Day 3 Retelling Assessment			Day 5 Fluency Assessment			Reteach	Teacher's Comments	Grouping
	The assessed group is highlighted for each week.	Benchmark Score	Actual Score	*The assessed group is highlighted for each week.*	Benchmark wcpm	Actual Score			
WEEK 1	**Hatchet** Sequence						✓		
	Strategic	1–2		Strategic	Less than 125				
	On-Level	3		On-Level	125–132				
	Advanced	4		Advanced*	125–132				
WEEK 2	**When Marian Sang** Generalize								
	Strategic	1–2		Strategic	Less than 125				
	On-Level	3		On-Level	125–132				
	Advanced	4		Advanced*	125–132				
WEEK 3	**Learning to Swim** Sequence								
	Strategic	1–2		Strategic	Less than 125				
	On-Level	3		On-Level	125–132				
	Advanced	4		Advanced*	125–132				
WEEK 4	**Juan Verdades** Generalize								
	Strategic	1–2		Strategic	Less than 125				
	On-Level	3		On-Level	125–132				
	Advanced	4		Advanced*	125–132				
WEEK 5	**Elizabeth Blackwell** Draw Conclusions								
	Strategic	1–2		Strategic	Less than 125				
	On-Level	3		On-Level	125–132				
	Advanced	4		Advanced*	125–132				
	Unit 3 Benchmark Test Score								

- **RECORD SCORES** Use this chart to record scores for the Day 3 Retelling, Day 5 Fluency, and Unit Benchmark Test Assessments.

*Students in the advanced group should read above-grade-level materials.

- **RE-GROUPING** Compare the student's actual score to the benchmark score for each group level and review the *Questions to Consider*. Students may move to a higher or lower group level, or they may remain in the same group.

- **RETEACH** If a student is unable to complete any part of the assessment process, use the weekly Reteach lessons for additional support. Record the lesson information in the space provided on the chart. After reteaching, you may want to reassess using the Unit Benchmark Test.

Assessment and Regrouping Chart

Unit 4

	Day 3 Retelling Assessment		Day 5 Fluency Assessment			Reteach	Teacher's Comments	Grouping
	The assessed group is highlighted for each week.	Benchmark Score	Actual Score	The assessed group is highlighted for each week.	Benchmark WCPM	Actual Score	Reteach	
WEEK 1	*Into the Ice* Cause/Effect						✓	
	Strategic	1–2		Strategic	Less than 130			
	On-Level	3		On-Level	130–138			
	Advanced	4		Advanced*	130–138			
WEEK 2	*The Chimpanzees I Love* Author's Purpose							
	Strategic	1–2		Strategic	Less than 130			
	On-Level	3		On-Level	130–138			
	Advanced	4		Advanced*	130–138			
WEEK 3	*Black Frontiers* Cause/Effect							
	Strategic	1–2		Strategic	Less than 130			
	On-Level	3		On-Level	130–138			
	Advanced	4		Advanced*	130–138			
WEEK 4	*Space Cadets* Draw Conclusions							
	Strategic	1–2		Strategic	Less than 130			
	On-Level	3		On-Level	130–138			
	Advanced	4		Advanced*	130–138			
WEEK 5	*Inventing the Future* Author's Purpose							
	Strategic	1–2		Strategic	Less than 130			
	On-Level	3		On-Level	130–138			
	Advanced	4		Advanced*	130–138			
Unit 4 Benchmark Test Score								

- **RECORD SCORES** Use this chart to record scores for the Day 3 Retelling, Day 5 Fluency, and Unit 4 Benchmark Test Assessments.

*Students in the advanced group should read above-grade-level materials.

- **RE-GROUPING** Compare the student's actual score to the benchmark score for each group level and review the *Questions to Consider*. Students may move to a higher or lower group level, or they may remain in the same group.

- **RETEACH** If a student is unable to complete any part of the assessment process, use the weekly Reteach lessons for additional support. Record the lesson information in the space provided on the chart. After reteaching, you may want to reassess using the Unit Benchmark Test.

© Pearson Education

Name _____ **Date** _____

Assessment and Regrouping Chart Unit 5

Day 3 Retelling Assessment			Day 5 Fluency Assessment			Reteach	Teacher's Comments	Grouping
The assessed group is highlighted for each week.	Benchmark Score	Actual Score	*The assessed group is highlighted for each week.*	Benchmark WCPM	Actual Score			

WEEK 1

View from Saturday
Plot

	Benchmark Score	Actual Score		Benchmark WCPM	Actual Score	Reteach	Teacher's Comments	Grouping
Strategic	1–2		Strategic	Less than 135		✓		
On-Level	3		On-Level	135–144				
Advanced	4		Advanced*	135–144				

WEEK 2

Harvesting Hope
Fact/Opinion

Strategic	1–2		Strategic	Less than 135				
On-Level	3		On-Level	135–144				
Advanced	4		Advanced*	135–144				

WEEK 3

River to the Sky
Cause/Effect

Strategic	1–2		Strategic	Less than 135				
On-Level	3		On-Level	135–144				
Advanced	4		Advanced*	135–144				

WEEK 4

Gold
Main Idea

Strategic	1–2		Strategic	Less than 135				
On-Level	3		On-Level	135–144				
Advanced	4		Advanced*	135–144				

WEEK 5

The House of Wisdom
Sequence

Strategic	1–2		Strategic	Less than 135				
On-Level	3		On-Level	135–144				
Advanced	4		Advanced*	135–144				

Unit 5 Benchmark Test Score _____

- **RECORD SCORES** Use this chart to record scores for the Day 3 Retelling, Day 5 Fluency, and Unit Benchmark Test Assessments.

*Students in the advanced group should read above-grade-level materials.

- **RE-GROUPING** Compare the student's actual score to the benchmark score for each group level and review the *Questions to Consider*. Students may move to a higher or lower group level, or they may remain in the same group.

- **RETEACH** If a student is unable to complete any part of the assessment process, use the weekly Reteach lessons for additional support. Record the lesson information in the space provided on the chart. After reteaching, you may want to reassess using the Unit Benchmark Test.

Assessment and Regrouping Chart

Unit 6

	Day 3 Retelling Assessment		Day 5 Fluency Assessment		Reteach	Teacher's Comments	Grouping
	The assessed group is highlighted for each week.		The assessed group is highlighted for each week.				
	Benchmark Score	Actual Score	Benchmark WCPM	Actual Score			
WEEK 1 — **Don Quixote** Author's Purpose					✓		
Strategic	1–2		Less than 140				
On-Level	3		140–150				
Advanced	4		Advanced* 140–150				
WEEK 2 — **Ancient Greece** Graphic Sources							
Strategic	1–2		Less than 140				
On-Level	3		140–150				
Advanced	4		Advanced* 140–150				
WEEK 3 — **The All-American Slurp** Compare/Contrast							
Strategic	1–2		Less than 140				
On-Level	3		140–150				
Advanced	4		Advanced* 140–150				
WEEK 4 — **The Aztec News** Draw Conclusions							
Strategic	1–2		Less than 140				
On-Level	3		140–150				
Advanced	4		Advanced* 140–150				
WEEK 5 — **Opportunity Awaits** Generalize							
Strategic	1–2		Less than 140				
On-Level	3		140–150				
Advanced	4		Advanced* 140–150				
Unit 6 Benchmark Test Score							

- **RECORD SCORES** Use this chart to record scores for the Day 3 Retelling, Day 5 Fluency, and Unit Benchmark Test Assessments.

*Students in the advanced group should read above-grade-level materials.

- **RE-GROUPING** Compare the student's actual score to the benchmark score for each group level and review the *Questions to Consider*. Students may move to a higher or lower group level, or they may remain in the same group.

- **RETEACH** If a student is unable to complete any part of the assessment process, use the weekly Reteach lessons for additional support. Record the lesson information in the space provided on the chart. After reteaching, you may want to reassess using the Unit Benchmark Test.